C000252418

THE VERY BEST OF
VOLKSWAGEN

THE VERY BEST OF
VOLKSWAGEN

Edited by Trevor Legate

TOUCHSTONE
BOOKS LTD

First published in 2006 by Touchstone Books Ltd

Touchstone Books Ltd
Highlands Lodge
Chartway Street
Sutton Valence
Kent ME17 3HZ
United Kingdom

www.touchstone-books.com

Copyright © Touchstone Books Ltd 2006

All rights reserved. No part of this publication may be reproduced, stored in a
retrieval system, or transmitted in any form or by any means, without the prior
written permission of the copyright holder.

A copy of the CIP data for this book is available from the British Library
upon request.

The rights of Trevor Legate to be identified as the author of this work have been
asserted in accordance with Section 77 of the Copyright, Designs and Patents Act
of 1988.

Designed by Paul Turner and Sue Pressley
Editorial consultants: Mike Pye and Nick Wigley

Printed and bound in Singapore

The author and publishers have made every reasonable effort to contact all copyright
holders. Any errors that may have occurred are inadvertent and anyone who for any
reason has not been contacted is invited to write to the publishers so that a full
acknowledgement may be made in subsequent editions of this work.

ISBN: 0-9551020-2-2

All images reproduced under licence
from VolksWorld, © IPC Media Limited

Picture credits:

Glyn Barney: 46/47
Stefan Bau: 20/21, 100/101
Bo Bertilsson: 48/49, 50/51
Kiki De Bois: 56/57, 58/59, 74/75, 76/77,
   96/97, 106/107, 112/113, 122/123,
   124/125, 128/129
Chris Brown: 14/15, 24/25
Gerrard Brown: 104/105
Tony Butler: 42/43, 62/63, 64/65, 118/119
John Colley: 10/11
Dave Fetherston: 16/17, 54/55, 78/79,
   108/109
James Hale: 120/121
Zoe Harrison: 2, 3, 30/31, 70/71, 82/83,
   84/85, 86/87, 92/93, 110/111
Norman Hodson: 40/41, 44/45
Masatake Ishiko: 52/53
Neil Pickett: 88/89
Steve Seal: 22/23, 116/117
Keith Seume: 28/29
Tom Silsbury: 114/115
Split Image: 66/67, 72/73, 80/81, 102/103
Chris Taylor: 68/69, 90/91

Touchstone Books Ltd – A winning combination
Inspired by creativity, driven by enthusiasm, and fuelled by passion!

The team: Trevor Legate is a talented professional photographer, motoring enthusiast, and
respected author. As professional graphic designers Paul Turner and Sue Pressley have a
long-established reputation for expertise in creating innovative and beautiful books. With
20 years experience in the world of corporate communications, Nick Wigley, a successful
historic race car driver, brings creative thinking and entrepreneurial flair to the mix.

Contents

Introduction 6
Beautiful in Blue 8
Taylor Made 10
First Class 12
Terminal Velocity 14
Rodbuster 16
Plum Crazy 18
Karmann Carrera 20
Pastel Perfect 22
Pacewagen 24
One of a Kind 26
Super Street Samurai 28
Hi-Tech Hauler 30
Blood Brothers 32
Yumbox 34
The Finest '56 36
On Safari 38
Candy Cabriolet 40
Pretty Green 42
Factory Fresh 44
Super Beetle 46
Custom Commercial 48
Already Salted 50
Art Attack 52
Home From Home 54
Purple Rain 56
Lowering Arizona 58
Wolfsburger King 60
House of Colours 62
Pap-ulance 64
Burn Baby Burn! 66

Shave It All Off 68
Contemporary Cruiser 70
Star Trekker 72
Bad '54 74
2 Cool 4 School 76
Thin is in 78
Viva Mexico! 80
Jean Genius 82
Dream Car 84
Surprise Surprise 86
Das Kool Bulli 88
Clockwork Orange 90
Gran Turismo 92
Arachnophobia 94
Hit the Beach 96
Sunshine Bus 98
The Right Stuff 100
Karmann Chameleon 102
Cool Water 104
Bhp Central 106
Counting Coppers 108
Split Screen Angels 110
21st Century Toy 112
Import Export 114
Summer Fun 116
Wide Boy 118
Leader of the Pack 120
'63 and Single 122
Muller Love 124
A Special Vintage 126
Purple Power 128

Introduction

THE VOLKSWAGENS of the air-cooled period, the rear engined Volkswagens such as the Type 1 (Beetle and Karmann Ghia), Type 2 (The Van, Pick up, Bus, Kombi, etc) and Type 3 (Saloon, Estate, Fastback and Karmann Ghia.) were the most surprising success story of the automotive industry. The Beetle was very nearly lost in the ashes of the bombed factory, which had been built specifically to produce the People's Car in Wolfsburg, Germany, at the end of World War II. Production plans had been shelved during the war to make way for production of military vehicles and equipment and this in turn had made the factory a target. Thanks to the occupying forces of the British military, who saw hope for the People's Car when others who felt they knew better had shunned it, the car was put into production after the war. By 1949 the Volkswagen factory had been handed back to Germany and the goal became to export the car to bring much needed foreign currency into the Germany economy. After a storming sales success in the United States, the Beetle went on to be the most popular vehicle in the world.

The success was based on an honest, reliable car with fabulous after sales service and spare parts back up. It changed little in looks, unlike many models which changed drastically in appearance every year or so, especially in the United States. A Beetle could be updated, the parts were easily interchangeable, and to a layman it was hard to tell the year, but it was very easy to tell what car it was from the silhouette. This helped make the car the most universally recognized car of all time, and the most used in advertising, too.

There is a massive enthusiast following for classic Volkswagens today, and as has always been the case, it is not limited to any country in particular – it is a worldwide phenomenon, large enough to warrant annual events and gatherings in numerous countries. The internet is bristling with websites and forums devoted to VWs, and the following is gaining in strength. It really doesn't matter whether you want a VW Beetle as your daily transport or an original classic Beetle which is cosseted and stored away, apart from the odd drive on a sunny day, or to enter into a concours d'elegance, or merely improve the performance or looks of the car; the Beetle is the most adaptable vehicle ever created. But in recent years, the versatile Bus has grown in popularity as its subtle charms have come to be appreciated by a new, younger group of enthusiasts who are not always impressed by the bland offerings from the modern car giants. And who can resist the timeless appeal of the stylish Karmann Ghia?

These classic VWs, unlike new cars, are easy to work on, even if you have little mechanical knowledge. All you need is a good manual; some basic tools and a bit of spare time – and perhaps the ability to regrow the skin of your knuckles every now and again. The fact the air-cooled VWs are so easy to work on has meant they have become the favourite car for many to modify, personalize or customize.

The VW scene, as it is known, is unlike anything else in the automotive world and since 1987 *VolksWorld* magazine has been at the forefront of this scene, observing and informing while featuring photographs and technical details of some of the best customized and restored air-cooled VWs from around the world. I have enjoyed being behind the editorial desk for a large proportion of the magazine's illustrious history and am delighted to see some of the finest cars and best photography gathered together in book form. Within this book, you will see some of the most significant VWs restored or customized over the last 19 years and follow the change of styles and fashion. (The first car to appear in this book was our 'feature' car in the first issue of *VolksWorld*) Whilst styles may change, there's little doubt the level of dedication and quality of worksmanship has got better and better, and will continue to do so. This book has been created to give you a unique insight into the VW scene, and if you like what you see, why not join in the fun – I can assure you that you will not regret it!

Ivan McCutcheon – Editor *VolksWorld*

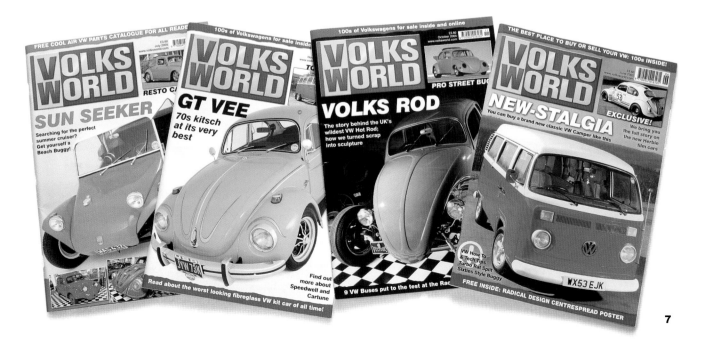

Beautiful in Blue

IN 1987, *VolksWorld* arrived on the magazine stands for the first time and one of its featured cars was this beautifully restored 1953 Oval Window Beetle which they described as 'Beautiful in Blue'. Its beauty was more than just skin deep for it had won the most prestigious award at the 1987 Bug Jam where it was confirmed as 'Europe's Most Beautiful VW'. To win the most coveted prize this side of the Atlantic had taken just six months of hard, dedicated work that transformed a tatty, rusting wreck into one of the finest examples of the world's classic automobiles.

To restore any vehicle to this standard requires a high level of skill and craftsmanship. Its owner worked for the Sussex-based international auto-design consultants, IAD, so the necessary skills were easily sourced and the access to such advanced facilities enabled the work to be carried out in record time. The pale blue paintwork was of the highest order and the interior was trimmed in two-tone grey and the matching carpets were hand sewn in dove grey wool.

When *VolksWorld* magazine first appeared on the scene, this Beetle was judged to be the finest example in Europe. Although times and tastes have evolved, good craftsmanship never dates. It's the attention to detail that sets such cars apart from the rest.

Taylor Made

S O YOU suddenly realize that you have access to more than adequate funds to purchase any car you wish or extend your current automotive collection in any way you see fit. A trip to the local supercar showroom is far from cool, so how about taking on an interesting challenge instead? Someone offers you a standard lhd '60 double cab that never came with a roof or corner windows – or four doors. The challenge was to combine this with a Barndoor Samba roof just 'to see if it could be done'. To cut a very long story short, it could, but not without considerable work. The *piece de resistance* to this creation was the addition of the fourth door; this required a new door aperture, internal strengtheners and a modified rhd door with hand-made handles inside and out. The clients brief to the restoration shop was to build it as Rolls Royce might have done and this is certainly reflected in every aspect of the vehicle, especially the interior. The Recaro seats and doors are finished with special cream leather, the rear seat is a split and widened Recaro, the floors trimmed with cream Wilton carpet and the headliner in West of England cloth. Down among the greasy bits, the 2276cc engine is coaxed to give 186bhp, driven through a five-speed Gene Berg 'box. Finished in Porsche rose metallic silver with a contrasting bronze upper section, this Taylor-made bus is a testament to British craftsmanship.

For the majority of VW enthusiasts, restoration is carried out with a close eye on the bank balance, since to do the job properly will always cost more than the original budget. However, it never hurts to stand back and admire a resto-project where finance was not a consideration – the quality of workmanship speaks for itself.

First Class

IF YOU were lying awake wondering what the world's finest Karmann Cabriolet looked like, worry no more for here it is. The Sussex-based owner of this remarkable rarity had previously agreed with his European-based agent that if and when an example surfaced, he would immediately buy it and restore it to as-new condition. This rare April 1952 'Split-dash' Karmann suffered front and rear damage in the '60s and was stored in southern Germany for over thirty years before word of its existence surfaced. Naturally, it was purchased on the spot and the two-year restoration saw over one thousand hours of labour lavished on the body alone; the damaged front bonnet you see before you is the original, beaten back to its correct shape by hand, with no trace of the repair work. Many of the unique features of this model remained in place but those that were missing were replaced with 'new old stock' items sourced from around the world, such as the chrome-finished aluminium wing beading with cloth dividing strips and an original wiring loom discovered in the USA. Every aspect of the car was restored to a standard, never down to a price; even the many coats of thin nitro-cellulose paint were mixed to original specifications, despite the tendency to crack over time. A Becker Monza radio was installed, plus a Hazet tourist spare wheel tool kit. In fact this car features over 20 ultra-rare accessories, including the solid aluminium grab handle mounted above the glovebox. This item was made especially for Split Cabriolets and features the grooved design of the door handles. Naturally, this truly perfect Cabriolet will be staying with its owner forever.

Never let it be said that 1952 was not a vintage year for VWs – this totally perfect Karmann Cabriolet has a timeless elegance that appeals to anyone with a soul. It helps if you can afford the cost of a restoration such as this, but lucky for us there are people who can.

Terminal Velocity

FEW PEOPLE would argue that the Type 34 Razor Edge Karmann Ghia is one of the most radical shapes to have escaped from the Volkswagen empire. Nor that the riot of shapes and angular lines lend themselves well to the world of Custom Car creations and spectacular paintjobs. This car was one of a pair purchased to create one really special Ghia (that became the Pagan Princess – don't you love cars with names?) and this was the wreck that served as a source of parts, having once suffered a monumental front end shunt earlier in its life. However, razor edge Ghias are not thick on the ground and, with the first car complete, it seemed a crime to leave this one to rot. Inspired by another famous VW, the Iguana, the reptilian theme seemed to offer interesting possibilities.

The Type 34 remains one of the great shapes from the Karmann collaboration as this stripped-out racer clearly demonstrates. And it's always good to see something different at the drag strip!

Thus the remarkable transformation began, from rusting wreck to a stripped-out race car that could be used on the road. This in itself was remarkable, but to complete the job in three months is hardly credible. It was decided not to destroy the original shape, letting the stunning 'fade' paint scheme do the talking. In went a 2276cc motor while the body was stripped, de-rusted and re-assembled for maximum lightness. Everything that could be drilled had holes added – even the decklid hinges. The body was sprayed in House of Kolors Lime Gold, Lime Time Pearl and Plant Green in 16 different shades to give the full fade effect. This was then overpainted with Sherwood Green, rag-rolled with Lime Gold Kandy mixed into the final lacquer coats. After 100 hours of labour, the paintwork was completed and, straight from its restoration, it ran 13-second quarters at the drag strip.

Rodbuster

RODBUSTER IS an example of the Beetle in Hot Rod form. The car has an interesting and diverse history; the project was initiated by Denny and Dale Jones of D&B Specialists in Van Buren, Arkansas where the majority of the work was carried out before it was sold to Terry Maheuron who completed it in Florida. The bodywork was acquired from a '61 Beetle convertible which was installed onto a '71 floorpan and running gear. The suspension was reset with a JC Performance beam axle featuring Sway-A-Way adjusters with Jaytech forged offset dropped spindles, disc brakes and Bilstein coil over shocks. Naturally, all suspension parts were chromed. The windscreen was lowered five inches and a black fabric top designed to fit. Power remained as a stock 1600cc unit with twin 34ICT Webers. Rectangular headlamps gave the car a distinctive look, as did the reversed 'suicide' doors and Pontiac Fiero headrest-speaker seats with matching grey trim and Mercedes cloth carpet, setting off the impressive lipstick red paintwork.

To some, the stuff of nightmares, to others, a work of genius. Whatever camp you are in, you have to admire the off-the-wall approach of the Rod guys. And it goes without saying that a Beetle-based Rod has a certain charm of its own. But be honest – you have always longed to own a VW with suicide doors!

Plum Crazy

THIS IMPRESSIVE Beetle is the result of plenty of hard graft, chrome, paint and an abandoned VW dragged from the proverbial farmer's field. Once the princely sum of £85 had changed hands, the gently rotting '72 1300cc Beetle departed the farm, its engine firing into life at the first time of asking. Although the mechanics were sound, the ferrous oxide had been working overtime. A bit of crafty welding and several coats of Hammerite applied to the floorpan sorted the problem and a seven-part Baja body kit topped it off. The engine was kept standard, other than the addition of 1600cc barrels and pistons, and a pair of Kadron carbs and Aeroquip hoses gave everything a professional look. Inside, all unnecessary trim was ripped out and everything was painted black including the dash that sports a bright fluorescent green speedo, a steering wheel sourced from a Porsche 928 and Hunter bucket seats. The matter of paintwork was a serious issue and hours spent trawling through paint swatches eventually unearthed the requisite shade from the Nissan range, imaginatively called Dark Red Metallic. Fortunately it looks a hundred times better than it sounds. The car was built to be used as a daily driver, but a very generous financial offer saw it change hands shortly after completion.

For fun on road or quarry, a Beetle has to be the car of choice. All it takes is a little imagination, some hard graft and a big pot of paint to create a bespoke automobile.

Karmann Carrera

FORTUNATELY A small, dedicated band of petrol heads still exist who consider the task of creating the ultimate car to be worth investing a considerable amount of their time and money. In the case of this German-owned Karmann Ghia, its owner required high levels of performance for travelling the autobahns and decided that the answer lay in Porsche power. Not just any Porsche engine, but a 3.6-litre 321-horsepower lump from a 993. This was never going to be a 'cheap' conversion but the result is a testament to what can be achieved. Great attention was paid to the suspension and brakes with parts sourced from 944, 993 and 996 models, plus the addition of factory ABS. Transmission came from a 993 with an RS differential, while the driver is located in a carbon-Kevlar racing seat. The most subtle modification was the elegant manner in which the coachbuilt bodywork was carefully pulled and moulded over the wheel arches and the bodywork was coated in a suitable shade of silver, from the Porsche Cayenne colour chart. The end result is a truly fabulous Ghia with a top speed of 186mph and the ability to stop and handle like a 911. It could be said that the original Ghia's lacked the performance levels that their appearance implied. Such a claim cannot be levelled at this example!

Pastel Perfect

DON'T BE fooled by this Beetle – a lot of subtle modifications have been carried out, but every time you cast your eyes over the bodywork, it's the lilac paintwork that attracts the attention. Few people would ever consider painting their prized possession in such a subtle pastel colour as VW's milka violet, but they would be missing a trick. The saga of Alison's 'California' VW began when she sold her boring shopping car and handed over £500 for this 1200cc 1973 Bug. Since her boyfriend was a builder of Hot Rods, he was volunteered to carry out the conversion work, beginning with a body-off restoration. Along the way, the tired old motor was ditched in favour of a Weber-fed 1641cc engine. When the body was re-fitted it was de-guttered and, to give a more 'vintage' appearance, the front wings were replaced with pre-68 items and a 'W' deck lid installed at the rear. Some careful de-chroming and lowering all round helped the overall appearance and a set of Porsche 356 replica wheels worked wonders. Inside, J Bugs grey velour seat covers and trim panels and grey carpeting are the height of good taste, set off by the exterior lilac paint that extends across the dashboard with the speedo finished in a paler shade of lilac. Never discount the 'pastel' car!

They laughed when they heard it was going to be a lilac Beetle, but on a car as smooth as this it looks very good indeed.

Pacewagen

THERE YOU are, with your hard-earned cash blown on your fancy Porsche Boxster and suddenly, in your mirrors, you spy a blue VW Bus. And it won't go away. As it powers past, it sounds like a Porsche and goes like a Porsche, which is understandable since where the old motor used to reside, this one now sports 2.7-litre Stuttgart power. Not just the engine and gearbox either, for this transformation swallowed the entire rear 911 section – torsion beams, shock mounts, axles, hubs, brakes, the lot. It all sounds relatively straightforward but (you guessed) details of this transplant would fill this book. Fortunately, this 1962 Swedish import is owned by a specialist Porsche mechanic who understood the potential pitfalls. He required family transport that could be used for long trips and holidays, where a top speed in excess of 60mph was desirable, but without resorting to using a highly-stressed engine to punch the decidedly un-aerodynamic shape through the air. Laws of physics dictate that it cannot be flung through corners in 911 fashion, but the final product is fast, reliable and a lot of fun. Nice!

Memorize the number plate and if you see this in your mirror, move over – it can shift! However, the party trick of this Bus is that was engineered correctly since it stops and handles as effectively as it accelerates.

One of a Kind

IN THE 1950s, the German coachbuilding company Hebmuller was noted for its conversions, modifying humble Beetle salons into stylish two-seater roadsters. Unable to locate a suitable Hebmuller, the original owner of this one-off car purchased a standard Beetle in September 1952 and delivered it to the small coachbuilding company, Stoll GmbH, with a request to turn it into a coupe. In spite of the shortened roofline, the car remained a full four-seater and even retained the storage space behind the rear seat. The larger, re-styled rear deck lid allowed easier access to the engine bay. The whole process was far from simple and it was 1954 before Stoll delivered the finished car to its owner. It remained in his possession until 1969 when he sold it to some American tourists. The trail goes cold around that time although it is known that the car had covered some 370,000 kilometres before it was discovered in London in a semi-derelict state. A VW enthusiast realized what he had found and money changed hands but, when the cost of restoration was established, it changed hands a few more times until it came into the possession of an owner was capable of undertaking the work. As an important piece of VW history, the job was carried out correctly with many 'new old stock' items unearthed, such as the front axle and all dashboard items. The original Webasto sunroof was renovated, the interior trimmed in Connolly leather and the car resprayed in the original two-tone style, using appropriate shades of beige and ivory. The rear window was the most expensive item, being a one-off as the original was thought to have come from a BMW501. However, this unique Stoll coupe has proved to be worth all the time and trouble and now resides in VW's own museum in Wolfsburg.

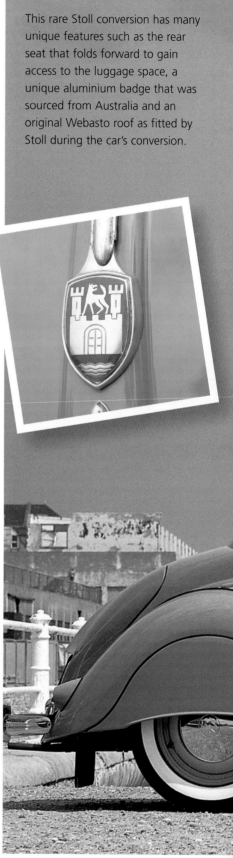

This rare Stoll conversion has many unique features such as the rear seat that folds forward to gain access to the luggage space, a unique aluminium badge that was sourced from Australia and an original Webasto roof as fitted by Stoll during the car's conversion.

Super Street Samurai

THE GHIA you see before you was transformed from a 1970 Karmann coupe into this wild PRA (Pro Racing Association) race car in a mere nine weeks, about one fifth of the usual development time. That, however, was the request made to Jimmy Larsen of JCL Racecars, in California, by his Japanese client. The challenge was accepted, a Ghia sourced and rapidly stripped to its component parts. To compete in the PRA Super Street class, the original floorpan had to be retained but considerable modifications were allowed to the suspension. At the rear, the torsion bar housing was shortened by 2.5 inches to allow 8-inch slicks to fit under the wheel arches. The client required the car to be right hand drive, as he intended to compete in Japanese PRA races, so the steering was swapped over and the roof lowered by three inches to meet the minimum height limit. While this work was under way, the engine was sent to Wik Racing Engines where the 2442cc motor was built from 94mm J & E pistons, chrome-moly cylinders and a super-light 88mm flanged crankshaft. Running with Gene Berg 58mm IDA carbs, the unit gave a very adequate 293bhp at 8500rpm. Final touches were a straight sequential transmission, a special rear deck lid with a huge rear wing and an eye-catching Bob Godfrey-sprayed paint job. And, no doubt, one very happy client.

This Super Street Ghia gets its power from an Adam Wik-built engine that punches out 293bhp @ 8500rpm thanks to an 88mm Scat crank, 94mm pistons, Sig Erson camshaft and Autocraft 910 series heads.

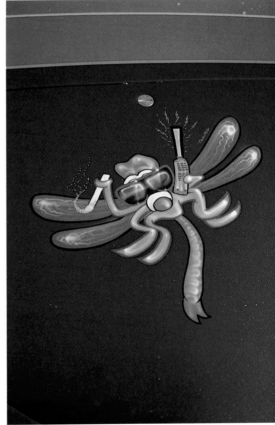

Hi-Tech Hauler

ONE OF the problems with starting any major restoration project is the temptation to go just that little bit further. And then a bit further still. And when you get that far, it's no real problem to gild the lily somewhat; it only requires money. And a bit more money. This 1200cc Bug was sourced from Belgium in a poor state. £500 changed hands but that sum purchased a sound 'shell and chassis, since most of the bolt-on bits were scrap. A quick overhaul brought it back to life as everyday transport but, as is often the case, a desire for more power, better brakes and a nicer interior proved too hard to resist. The Bug was destined to be transformed into a truly modern automobile, far more than just another VW with a big engine. The transformation was conducted from stem to stern; not only was it mounted onto Porsche Boxster 17-inch alloys, but behind those are four-wheel Kerscher discs, ventilated at the front, that are equal to the task of dissipating the power from the 2276cc engine. This features DTA fuel-injection with crank trigger ignition and punches out 173 horsepower on the dyno, a considerable increase over the original 34bhp motor. The cam is an Engle FK-87, a fairly wild piece of kit that could make the car a bit of a handful on the road were it not regulated by 45mm throttle bodies mounted onto match-ported CB manifolds and a DTA management module. The old interior was also upgraded with a pair of high-backed Recaro seats and the action is monitored with a full set of VDO gauges tastefully mounted in a custom-built dash.

The car runs on Avon low-profile rubber and was dropped by around 2.5 inches to give a better stance and ride height. CB dropped spindles were used at the front and re-set torsion bars at the rear, along with Koni shocks all round.

This is one tough Bug but the beauty is definitely more than skin deep – look past the Boxster wheels and you'll find four-wheel discs and a fuel-injected engine bolted to a five-speed transmission.

Blood Brothers

HERE, FOR your delight and delectation, we present an example of two minds thinking alike at the same time. During 1994, two people undertook the restoration and modification of two Karmann Ghia coupes and ended up with very similar vehicles, give or take a paint job. The red Ghia started life in 1966 and was purchased in a state of sad repair prior to its rebirth as shown, fully renovated and resprayed in its original colour. Both owners decided, independently, to add a set of EMPI-style five-spoke polished alloy wheels and lower the front suspension while leaving the rear stock in classic 'Cal-Look' style. The screaming-yellow Ghia is an rhd '68 model that was acquired at the same time as a Cal-Look Bug. The Bug donated much if its running gear to the Ghia while the Ghia parts went to the Bug. This was then sold to finance the Ghia project. This car then disappeared into a restoration workshop for eight months before it resurfaced as you see it here. The car also received a 2110cc motor, created in the USA, while the red Ghia continues to make use of its original 1600cc stock motor. The red machine inherited American-spec 'towel-rail' front and rear bumpers that, for the colour blind, help to distinguish it from its 'blood brother'.

Yumbox

YES, YOU spotted it straight away – this Beetle is not a product from the production line in downtown Wolfsburg in Germany. As you correctly surmised, it originated from the Puebla plant in Mexico, but it has changed its appearance quite radically since 1982, having been involved in an accident in 1988. The wreck was purchased by a Volkswagen repair specialist who knew how to right the wrongs and, by the time the welding torch was put away, YUM 80X was a red street car, lowered and fitted with EMPI eight-spoke wheels. Shortly afterwards, it was granted a Bergman 2.3-litre motor that was strong enough to record a 13.10 second run at the Santa Pod dragstrip. Thus the racing bug bit hard and some serious tinkering began. To document such work would fill half this book, but suffice it to say that a VW camper was sold to pay for the carbs and a Karmann Cabriolet had to go in exchange for the cylinder heads. Using 94mm Venolia racing pistons, the engine displacement was enlarged to 2387cc. Wheels were supplied by Centreline and the 7x15s rear are shod with 26x8x15 Goodyear slicks. Such dedication and financial outlay resulted in the car covering the quarter-mile in 10.34 seconds at 130mph.

Although Yumbox is an out-and-out racer, it remains just about streetable, although there are better VWs to use on the shopping run.

It all fits in there somehow *(left)*! The engine features an 86mm Scat flanged crankshaft with 94mm Venolia pistons. The carbs are massive 62mm JayCee Terminators. And in true race style, it all comes apart very easily *(above)*. The ideal tool for a 10.34 second quarter-mile blast *(below)*.

The Finest '56

IF YOU belong to the group of owners who do not subscribe to the theory of customizing, Hot-Rodding or race-preparing your VW, the most critical aspect of ownership (or a restoration job) becomes originality. Once in a while, a VW surfaces that has this quality in spades, although the older they are, the more likely that parts have gone missing or been replaced with, shall we say, inferior items. The owner of this 1956 Karmann convertible spent two years negotiating its purchase before he met with success. He knew he had obtained a rare classic that still had all its original components, even down to the headlight rims that still had 'Bosch' embossed on them. All that was needed was to strip the car back to its component parts (photographing the process to assist reassembly) and clean and de-rust as required. As oil had been used as a preservative on the floorpan, it was in 'as new' condition and the seat covers were excellent, these being the hardest items to match if one required replacing. Once the convertible came back together, the final flourish was a paint job of strato silver blue metallic, lacquered with ICI two-pack. A new navy mohair hood was created, but the original rubber floor mats were undamaged. Many people questioned the unusual black wheels, but the factory records confirmed that they had been ordered from new. Beneath the vented 'W' rear deck lid lies the original engine, now rebuilt and running better than ever as this classic VW enjoys a new lease of life.

The fuel tank sits happily behind the spare wheel *(right)* and was painted blue when it left the factory 50 years ago. If you brought a Karmann Cabriolet between 1956 and 1959, this is the steering wheel you would have become familiar with *(below right)*. The car looks even more stylish with the mohair roof stowed.

On Safari

SPLIT-SCREEN campers have always been a popular choice for major custom projects and wild flights of the imagination, but fascinating as such creations are, it's always a delight to come across a clean, sympathetically restored original. This 1962 'splittie' came into the possession of a new owner who decided it was the ideal antidote to his motorcycle addiction and a way of preserving his endangered driving licence. With the aerodynamic qualities of Buckingham Palace and an 1192cc engine that had seen service for 275,000 miles, the top speed of 60mph was just the job! The safari-windowed camper had fortunately been cared for by a sympathetic owner who had kept it in the family for the first 26 years of its life. Inevitably, however, the insidious rot had been at work around the nether regions and some welding and cutting was required before the refreshed bodywork was sprayed with lotus white above and Toyota pastel blue below. It was soon back in use as a daily driver so refurbishment of the interior, assembled by the first owner, was delayed until *VolksWorld* magazine requested the pleasure of its company at the annual Sandown Park show. A quick overhaul and some gentle varnishing returned this well-used split-window to its original splendour.

If ever there was a vehicle that conjures up warm summer days and a soundtrack of Beach Boys songs, it has to be a blue and white Splittie. With its beautifully constructed interior, original engine, a mere quarter of a million miles on the clock and spiffing whitewall tyres, this VW begs to be driven to the nearest beach.

Candy Cabriolet

WHEN THE owner of this 1973 Karmann cabriolet saw it for the first time it was sitting in a dealers showroom in Sussex, having just arrived from the USA, and he was in no position to buy it. He took a photograph instead and thought that was the end of the story until, two years later, their paths crossed again. The car was once again for sale and this time it would not get away. Although it was generally in good condition, he decided that his special car should be even more special, so a series of restorative measures were undertaken. Top of the list was the choice of an appropriate colour before the car departed for its full repaint. The selection of dark cherry pearl from the Chrysler range proved just about perfect, as can be seen. Rather than opt for the usual black roof, a new canvas top in contrasting red proved to be a successful decision and the dark red theme extended to the new carpet set. The rather ordinary 'safety' steering wheel was replaced by an earlier example with the semi-circular horn push and various tasteful accessories, such as the very appropriate Sprintstar wheels, have been added to create a truly desirable soft-topped Beetle.

Motive power for this tasteful Cabriolet is a Type 1 1584cc engine, fed via a centre-mounted Dell 'Orto 40DRLA carb on a non-plenum manifold. Serious thought went into this beautifully crafted VW that is every bit as perfect inside as out – even the greasy bits received the same attention to detail.

Pretty Green

PART OF the challenge in restoring a Beetle to 'as new' condition is sourcing as many original, or 'new old stock' (NOS) items as possible to bestow that identifiable stamp of authenticity and quality to the finished product. This 1300cc model, that rolled off the Emden production line in 1975, is the result of a year-long complete nut and bolt rebuild to that level. The Beetle's owner was an aircraft engineer who always wanted to take on a restoration project when time allowed and the end result is a reflection of his dedication and craftsmanship. A lot of hard graft was required, since 20 years of use on British roads had to be cleaned off the rolling chassis, plus some restoration to some earlier accident damage, but a lot of elbow grease and a little welding, plus copious amounts of Waxoyl, put things back in showroom condition. Every part was cleaned or replaced with a genuine item and the body was repainted in two-pack lofoten green and oven baked. Sensible upgrades were deemed acceptable, such as an electric washer pump and halogen bulbs in the headlamps. The Securit heated rear window and Hella fog lamp were retained since they were contemporary accessories. A restoration such as this also serves to demonstrate to owners why so many Beetles survive for so long, thanks to a policy of simple construction and the use of good quality materials.

As this Beetle rolled off the production line, VW unveiled the first Golf. Twenty years later, the MkIII Golf arrived while the Beetle was treated to a sympathetic restoration, ready for another twenty years of service. In the tail, an AD-series engine was built to period-correct specification.

Factory Fresh

THIS BEAUTIFUL amazon green Ghia started life in Waco, Texas, after leaving the Osnabruck factory in 1959. Its first owner averaged 8,300 miles a year for ten years before it was put into hibernation in a barn for a further 16 years. In 1985, it emerged with a new owner and a red colour scheme inside and out. Its next owner contacted the Karmann Ghia Owners Club in the UK for advice, which was freely given by the secretary of the Type 1 Registry. As a result of their correspondence, he ended up buying the car and importing it into the UK in 1992. Serious work began to return the car to its former glory, although the only welding work required was to replace the original dashboard that had been seriously abused in order to fit a huge and offensive radio. Although the car was built just one month prior to the factory offering right-hand drive Ghias, the new owner considered it acceptable to swap the steering over to the right in order to enjoy using it on British roads. The original colour was discovered on the back of the ashtray so this was sent to Germany where sufficient paint was mixed to respray the whole car. A new mohair hood was created but every other component was sourced as 'new old stock' wherever possible and the car retrimmed to the highest standards, with the asset of whitewall tyres topping off the '59 look.

There are few coupes as elegant an as early Karmann Ghia and this is one of the very best. Imported from the USA, it arrived with the original bill of sale and key that opens doors, glovebox and bonnet locks.

The 1584cc twin-port engine that powered the 1303S Beetle and produced 50bhp at 4000rpm.

Super Beetle

The optional 5.5Jx15 GT Sports wheels give the 1303S a slightly aggressive appearance.

T O TAKE the 'Best Original' award at the National *VolksWorld* Show requires something special and this 1974 1303S Super Beetle is just that – a stock unmolested and unrestored example. The only non-stock part is the stereo system, although eagle-eyed connoisseurs will question the non-standard 5.5Jx15 GT sports wheels, but these were ordered from the options list and were fitted to the car from day one. The 1303S came equipped with a 1584cc twin-port engine that gave 50bhp at 4000rpm. Also, it came with MacPherson front suspension, independent at the rear, and a curved 'panoramic' windscreen, a plastic safety dashboard with through-flow ventilation plus adjustable louvred outlets. The Super Beetles were bigger than the torsion-bar Bugs; under the front hood they had 85 per cent more space due to a relocated spare wheel, while more space was available in the cockpit. However, the larger, heavier model was also quite thirsty, averaging around 25mpg. This car's first owner was a 21-year-old who desired a decent sound system, so in went a top of the range Pioneer stereo, but aside from that the basically standard car remained in his possession until the end of 1993 when it changed hands with just 21,000 miles on the clock. When the new owner took it to the Sandown show, many people mistook it for a great restoration job. This will be a 'sunny weekend' car that will remain as original as possible for as long as possible.

Custom Commercial

IN THE world of VWs, one of the more sought-after models is the '58 split-screen bus, the final year of 'ribbed' front bumpers before the factory switched to plain ones. To the purist, a '58 bus should be revered and restored to its original specification, but when this bus fell into the hands of two brothers in Germany, it resurfaced as a pristine example of their personal ideologies. One brother earned his living keeping the products of Wolfsburg on the road while the other was a custom car builder, more at home with American metal and '30s rods. The result is an amalgamation of their two worlds. Much of the four-year build was spent getting the body perfect, but originality was never top of the agenda; at the rear, a later tailgate was installed and the rear bumper deleted (a pre-1954 feature). Underneath, a new stock engine was installed and their Hot Rod skills brought in to drop the bus as low as possible using a '66 Type 3 rear axle and gearbox. Cutting and trimming the front beam, Koni shocks and custom power-assisted discs provide a highly efficient handling and stopping package. Naturally the paintwork was a critical factor and ICI gloss black was applied before a contrasting coat of magenta created a new striking design. This was beautifully outlined in white, which sounds simple, but needs a trained eye to get right. Inside, Mercedes-quality leather and wool was added to every surface along with an 11-speaker, 3-amp, CD sound system to keep the happy occupants entertained.

Custom paint, a custom aluminium front bumper and nipple hubcaps make this a very special Bus.

Already Salted

THIS BRIGHT red projectile was built with one purpose – to achieve the highest possible speed across a salt lake. Owner Bob Stahl and his team in Huntington Beach, California, have been regularly setting speed records at all three lake races: El Mirage, Muroc and Bonneville. Needless to say, to create a Beetle that will run at speeds in excess of 150mph across a surface of salt requires a very special Bug indeed. Just slapping a huge engine in the rear will create a vehicle with the properties of the Space Shuttle, with similar re-entry problems. In contrast to drag racing, what is required is weight, but added in the right places. In this case, the light front end is kept in touch with terra firma by bolting heavy steel plates into the nose and, with a NASCAR-style rollcage, it tips the scales at 2500lb. Large disc brakes are fitted, but a parachute is desirable to keep the stopping distance at under one mile. This 1968 Bug originally ran with 2-litre power but now boasts a 2914cc lump built around a Type 4 crankcase with an 84mm crank and 105mm cylinders. It uses a 322-degree Isky cam with Scat Type 1 lifters, split-port heads, Manley valves, Berg springs and titanium retainers. The fuel-injection system uses Hilborn 3-inch throttle bodies plus port-injection which has built-in nozzles for the nitrous oxide system. First test runs produced speeds of 145-150mph prior to an attempt on the F/Altered class record of 162mph. More recently the team have achieved 157mph.

Under the bonnet of this Bonneville specialist lies fuel cells for petrol and methanol, NOS nitrous bottle, battery and lead weights to keep the nose in contact with the salt, while a parachute strapped to the tail helps slow the Bug from 157mph. The ballast required to balance the car means the fastest Bug is also the heaviest. Solid wheels and narrow tyres help the aerodynamics.

Art Attack

NO, YOUR eyes do not deceive you, nor is this an optical illusion. It really is a wrought-iron masterpiece created by some demented craftsman simply because he could. The history of this 'creation' is sketchy to say the least, but legend has it that it was created down Mexico way circa 1972. Quite why is another question; maybe for publicity purposes or as a result of an overdose of Colombian marching powder, but whatever the reason, it seems he built more than one! It may be that three of these 'Birdcage Beetles' exist, but nobody seems too certain. This example is cared for by the owner of the Flat Four company in Japan, while another is known to be in California. Whether this is the same car as the one owned by the late Vasek Polak, of Porsche fame, is unclear. This 'different' creation still has a place in a VW book (instead of an 'Unusual Garden Furniture' book) since beneath what passes for bodywork is a stock Beetle with a 1293cc engine and 70 miles on the clock. How it racked up that huge mileage is uncertain as its owner tried to drive it once and was scared silly by the body-flex. However, it would be amusing to import one into the UK just to watch your local MOT tester suffer a complete nervous breakdown. Great fun!

If you have a burning desire to be noticed, a birdcage Beetle is the answer. The headlights seem to float and engine access is second to none – imagine how much work went into this fantastic creation.

Home From Home

FOR THE dedicated Beetle owner who wants to travel but cannot bear the thought of leaving his beloved car at home, the SuperBugger provides the answer – take your home with you! The tale of this slightly bizarre creation dates back to the early 1970s when *Popular Mechanics* magazine in the USA offered a complete set of blueprints to build your own Beetle home. This example was developed and built by Super Campers in Costa Mesa in 1981 and is based on a 1973 1600cc Beetle, plus a further $12,000 worth of modifications. The donor was sawn off at the base of the windscreen and everything behind it was removed before a fully-framed body was attached to the floorpan. This wood and aluminium creation was insulated and reinforced so that the roof could accommodate extra luggage, while the interior was fitted out with fold-out beds, seating for four, a table, fridge and water storage tank. The front seats were located further back and allowed to rotate to create extra seating. The lightweight constructions added just 250lb to the vehicle's weight, but the compromised aerodynamics demanded the use of a 2110cc engine to help ascend steep hills. Super Campers anticipated a steady flow of orders, but only 15 were built and it is thought that just four survive – but it's the ultimate way to arrive at a Volkswagen show…

Not the unfortunate love-child of a Winnebago and a Bug but the answer to a question not many people had asked – the SuperBugger was created by Super Campers in California and fifteen examples took to the Interstate highways where, no doubt, they confused many motorists. It was not the most aerodynamic VW but it has a certain charm.

Purple Rain

IN THE world of modified automobiles, you can bet the Americans have a word for it – and in this case the word is 'Resto-Custom'. The other popular term is 'Resto-Cal' which is a car that is usually much closer to a stock VW, save for a lowering job and a handful of period goodies. These cars are happy running on stock wheels and making use of an 1192cc engine. Resto-Custom cars, such as this, come with decidedly non-standard paintwork, especially candy paint and eye-catching metallic finishes. This 1963 'Sunroof' Bug hails from Tempe, Arizona and was subjected to a mile-deep candy purple paint job (violet pearl) from the House of Kolors Shimrin range (how non-standard can you get?). Six coats of violet were sprayed over two of black before five coats of lacquer and some serious polishing created the final effect. In true custom tradition, underneath the body every part that was not rubber was either painted purple or chromed, while chrome was applied to the American Eagle wheels, bumper bars, over-riders, headlight rings and quarter-light windows. In the power department, the engine was united with a period supercharger kit built by Judson and an increase in capacity from 1192cc to 1385cc (see page 128). A custom-made exhaust system was created that exits just in front of the right hand side rear wheel.

Loaded with chrome and shiny bits, this Resto Custom Bug shines in the Arizona sun. In case you were wondering, that's a custom-made stainless steel snowboard rack on the roof – just in case it snows!

Lowering Arizona

WHEN IT comes to considering the Volkswagen scene in the USA, it is all too easy to think that the restoration and customizing business begins and ends in California. But like most preconceptions, it's never that straightforward as this gleaming Beetle from Glendale, Arizona, demonstrates. Without doubt, the SoCal VW scene is the largest in the States, but its neighbour, Arizona, runs it pretty close. One of the most dedicated members of the fraternity created this silver 'daily driver' from a '61 Bug that was fitted with a full-length sunroof (termed a 'ragtop' in American-speak). To ensure the required reliability, a lot of the greasy parts, including the motor, were left as stock, but the rest of the car was given the full Resto-Cal look. Silver bodywork with a red interior is not uncommon on Porsches, but the combination works just as well on a Beetle, so on went Porsche silver polaris two-pack and early-style seats were trimmed in red with matching carpets. To give the car a 'narrow' look, the front beam was shortened by four inches and dropped spindles were used, along with narrow 15-inch chromed-plated Fuchs wheels, just 4.5 inches wide. 6x15 inch Fuchs were installed at the rear where a pair of air shocks help create the nose-down look and can raise the ride height at will. Next time you're passing through Arizona, be sure to look out for this one.

Building a super-cool Resto-Looker isn't all about having a tyre-shredding motor – it's all about style. The recipe for creating a flawless result like this is to take one '61 Beetle with a full-length 'ragtop' sunroof, throw on some chromed Porsche rims, narrow it, slam it, paint it and drive it. But attention to detail is everything.

Wolfsburger King

IT MUST be pretty difficult to live in Wolfsburg – the home of Volkswagen – and not be afflicted by the VW bug (so to speak). Certainly the owner of this Cal-Look '53 Oval has given in to the inevitable, but he has not gone down the 'classic' route as he also likes to feel the power under his right foot. He purchased the '53 bodyshell from his brother and this was treated to new lower quarter panels, heater channels, bumper mounts and inner rear wings, as well as a shortened spare wheel well to allow the addition of a front-mounted oil cooler. All the trim holes were welded up and the inner rear wings modified to allow access to the carbs and spark plugs for tuning. The W-decklid had cabriolet-style louvres welded in. The bodywork was then mounted onto a later IRS floorpan, with ball-joint torsion bar front suspension and painted VW cherry red. Wheels were a critical choice and Fuchs alloys are always a firm favourite, 4.5Jx15 rims up front and 6Jx15 rear, shod with Firestone F-560 rubber. The front end was dropped using a Puma beam and long-travel ball joints, while the back was gently decambered by turning the torsion bars and spring plates on the inner and outer splines. For braking, Kerscher ventilated discs, using widened Type 3 calipers are well up to the job, with a Porsche 944 master cylinder employed to push the fluid around. But the all-important engine is a 1966cc stroker with 44IDF Webers and a trick 010-based electronic ignition system. It punches out close to 150bhp, more than sufficient for a bit of Beetle-based fun.

Under the bonnet (*opposite*), you'll find all kinds of tricks such as a shortened spare wheel well to accommodate a front-mounted oil cooler. Fuchs wheels look the business, while a set of Opel seats add a touch of comfort.

House of Colours

THIS STYLISH Split-screen may appear to be a cherished, customized family heirloom, but looks can be deceptive since this Bus does service as a daily driver. In fact, it is a rolling advertisement for one of the UK's premier custom vehicle painters, Prosign. It goes without saying that when you spray your own vehicle, the result has got to be perfect and the Prosign Bus is as good as it gets. It arrived in the UK in 2001 after a career in the German fire service and after the assorted blue lights were removed from the roof, a custom 'woody' paint job was applied that caused much debate as to whether it was real wood or paint (no prizes for guessing). However, for the 2004 show season, its owners decided a change of colour scheme was required, along with a general lowering of the ride height for that 'Surf-Bus' look. The debate as to whether to repaint the whole Bus was resolved by a home-alone wife and a can of paint-stripper (a dangerous combination). She had a firm idea of the new look though and after just two weeks of hard work, the Bus had a remarkable new roof design, created by using cut-out shapes of hibiscus flowers. Various shapes were removed as each layer of kandy apple red was sprayed on to vary the colours, while some flower patters received highlights while others had airbrushed drop-shadows for the full 3D effect. This flower motif was continued inside, on doors and floor, while the body colours of red and cream was complemented by a set of original whitewall tyres. The Prosign logos were the final touch, hand written and finished in gold leaf for the ultimate touch of class.

You don't have to have great artistic ability to design and produce a truly wonderful Bus – but if you do, just look at what can be created! Hot Rod surf Buses don't come much better than this fine example.

Pap-ulance

FOR THE benefit of those who are not well versed in the minutiae of VW history, the extremely rare vehicle you see on these pages is a coachbuilt conversion created by Karosserie Papler of Cologne in 1952. Papler were not the first to offer a four-door Cabriolet, as Hebmuller offered a similar vehicle (Type 18A) for police use as early as 1946. These first cars were pretty basic, with ropes instead of doors (!) and a rudimentary folding roof. Eventually the cars were built with doors and business was flourishing until a disastrous factory fire in 1949 resulted in the company going out of business three years later. Karosserie Papler took advantage of the situation and began supplying the police with their own cabriolet conversion, that was generally accepted as being better engineered. Unlike Hebmuller, Papler did not have an agreement regarding the supply of VW cars direct from the factory so they were forced to purchase used examples. It took two men two weeks to convert each car, each man working on one side As a result, the size of the doors on either side of the car was rarely the same! Around 500 cars were built and this example was used by the police until 1959 and then from 1961 to 1966 as a Red Cross vehicle in Recklinghausen. An accident saw it go into storage in 1970 until it was disinterred some 30 years later. The accident damage was carefully repaired and its new owner repainted it in its 'Red Cross' livery of white with red crosses instead of the more usual 'Police' green.

At the front of this rare Papler conversion is a genuine Red Cross spotlight, external horn and flashing indicators installed on the front wing, as the original semaphore indicators were lost when the door pillars were removed. Interior trim is basic but the construction is more solid than it appears and the doors shut with a solid clunk.

Burn Baby Burn!

WHEN YOU own a major VW parts business importing Gene Berg items into the UK, and are already responsible for building a couple of the finest VWs ever seen, what do you do for an encore? Having built a street-legal Bug that can return 11-second quarter-mile times (!) the only way forward is to create the ultimate race car. It was decided, after much beer and pizza, to build a car in tribute to the original Gene Berg black '67. With the approval of the Berg family in the States, the search began for the donor car. The simple solution would be to purchase an immaculate 1967 Beetle but it was considered sacrilege to destroy a sound car, especially since only the bodyshell was needed. Eventually, the right kind of tatty Bug turned up and was rapidly reduced to its component parts. This is where the saga gets complicated and technical since you do not just add a few quick bits onto what was left

Huge slicks, a stinger exhaust and wheelie bars hint that this is no road car, but for a drag car, the interior is positively luxurious with modified seats from a Lotus Elan and a gear shift moved five inches back.

and go racing. The project was carefully planned on a laptop, the right people were contacted to ensure the correct parts would be available and then the huge task of building a race car began. Over 700 man-hours were spent on the paint and body alone and, like the body, the floor was sandblasted before the primer was applied and a custom chromoly roll cage installed before final painting. The engine was built using many one-off components and rated at 2387cc, giving 214bhp, all driven via a custom-built Autocraft transmission. Wheels are replica BRMs although the rears are replaced with gold-anodized spun aluminium Ercos shod with Firestone slicks for use at the race track. Inside, everything is beautifully trimmed with a pair of customized Lotus seats and Simpson harnesses. Straight out of the box, the '67 ran an 11.8 second quarter-mile and achieved the owner's goal of a 10-second quarter in 2005.

Shave It All Off

IT MAY be hard to believe, but this remarkable, full-on custom Beetle started from a festering pile of scrap that used to be a 1968 1500 VW. The highlight of the original 'car' was the fact that the engine fired, but matters went downhill from there, as the two inches of water that occupied the interior suggested. When you start on a project to create one of the best custom Bugs in the UK, this is not a good place to start from. However, blind faith and a considerable pile of folding saw the arrival of a truckload of new body panels and the purchase of a Mexican floorpan saw to it that not a lot of the '68 Beetle survived the cut – but the owners had purchased a heavy duty sound system and they needed somewhere VW-shaped to install it. They also liked the idea of fitting a set of Ford Mondeo Ghia alloys, so considerable work was done to the front wings (that needed to be extended anyway to clear the Mercedes S-class headlights). A new set of custom running boards were fabricated and the roof de-guttered – very carefully, three inches at a time and welded as it was removed. The unique front-opening 'suicide' doors required considerable engineering expertise and were trimmed using Ford Ka inner door panels. Inside, the rear seat was sacrificed for the music as in went a Pioneer DAB CD radio-head unit, two Pioneer amps (1500 watts in total), three Rockford-Fosgate Punch XLC subs. Loud. Up front, a VW Caddy tailgate serves as a dashboard while the Dakota digital instruments live on the floor. The Cobra seats were trimmed in Ferrari Crema leather, while the body, suspension and most metal areas were sprayed in Spies Hecker citrine yellow paint, with the wheels finished in pearl white.

Suicide doors on a vehicle such as this –
it's a lemon entry my dear Watson!
Cobra sidewinder seats *(below)* are
a tasteful addition to one of
the most carefully thought-
out custom designs.

Contemporary Cruiser

THIS 1956 23-window Deluxe Microbus is a perfect example of a restoration carried out by one of the best VW restoration companies in the UK. The result of their efforts is a 100 per cent accurate recreation of how this humble Bus looked in 1956, but with paintwork that is far superior to anything from that period. It may be visually perfect, inside and out, but its secret lies beneath, since the client requested that this vehicle could be used reliably on today's busy roads. This means having an engine with sufficient power to cope with steep gradients and brakes that will do their job, rather than trust to luck. As with any such 100-point restoration, the art lies in the details; that and ensuring that the bodywork is perfectly straight before undertaking any major work. This Bus had been sourced from Sweden and only required new metalwork around the nose and rear corners, plus 'new old stock' cargo doors. Since these doors were not the correct year, in order to retain the correct period door handles, the metal around the old handles was cut away and grafted into the new doors. The still-original interior was totally refurbished and the bodywork painted chestnut brown over a sealing wax red lower half. All the windows received new rubber trim while the front drum brakes made way for more modern discs. The suspension was rebuilt with new gas dampers and a new 1600cc engine was bolted in. Finally the Samba was converted to 12amp electrics powered via an alternator.

There's no easy way to make a Split look straight – it's all down to hard work and a lot of that has gone into this project, resulting in an amazing 23-window Bus.

This Deluxe Microbus came with a top of the range interior, 1956-style. The seats and panels are all original; other than some re-stitching and some serious cleaning, they have survived the ravages of time.

Star Trekker

FOR THOSE good folk who desire a VW but are less than excited by the usual offerings, how about bringing a little Trekker into your life (or if you are American, a Thing)? The Type 181, or Mehrzweckwagen, to give it the correct title, is often mistakenly referred to as the Kubelwagen – the vehicle it was designed to replace thirty years later. What began as a military project turned into a civilian recreational vehicle that was far more successful in the USA than over here. On the other side of the Atlantic, the 181 was launched as a recreational vehicle in 1973 and was marketed as 'The Thing'. VW had wanted to call it the Safari, but Citroën had the rights to that, so 'Thing' was chosen by a panel. In Europe, the Germans still called it a Kubelwagen, while in the UK a competition was held to name the car and Trekker was voted the winner. Only UK-registered rhd (Type 182) models built to civilian specs were called Trekkers and only around 250 were registered. So if you want one, or can find one, you will pay a premium! Between 1969 and 1972, 181s were built in Germany while all later cars ('73 – '80) were built in Mexico. Whatever the year, it is advisable to check for rust problems on all cars, since many were never rust-proofed and all UK cars were built on Karmann Ghia floor panels which can prove expensive to replace. Most parts are Beetle or Ghia based, apart from the front hubs that feature a raised spindle mounting point. Engines were 1500cc in '69 and '70 models and 1600cc after that. The Trekker has its own unique appeal and, if you can find a sound example, it makes for unusual and economical transport even though, like all 'unique' vehicles, ownership can often prove a labour of love.

The folding roof of a Type 181 Trekker is best described as adequate and the flimsy sidescreens drop into the door tops with metal pins. Ground clearance is generous thanks to raised spindles. Interiors are designed for business not pleasure and echo the general spartan quality of the whole ensemble.

Bad '54

A FEW MOMENTS spent scanning the images on this page will convince you that there ain't no substitute for bling, nor that this feast of chrome and wild paint hails from Las Vegas, where bling is king. This humble 1954 Bug, replete with three-fold sunroof, was almost reduced to toast in a Nevada bush fire, which is how it came into the possession of the owner of Bugshack in Nevada. As a foremost exponent of all things VW, he knew precisely how to restore and customize a burnt out Oval for maximum effect, having built countless examples for his happy clients. All his accumulated know-how went into this Bad '54, not least the noticeable green colour scheme that extends across every surface, above and below, including the wheel arches, all set off with tasteful marbleized purple flames. Every component that could be chromed received the treatment, including an engine case polished to a mirror finish. The engine was certainly not neglected, with a Porsche fan conversion and carbon fibre fan housing. The 2276cc motor delivers 135bhp at 6500rpm with the aid of 48IDA Webers, ported cylinder heads and an Engle 110 camshaft. The wheels are a crucial part of the package and measure 18 inches up front, 20 rear, the latter just accommodating 245x35x20 tyres in the arches. Inside, Pontiac seats are trimmed in 'plum and malibu sand' tweed cloth with the Bad 54 logo embossed on the backs. Naturally a high-output DVD and stereo system complete the package with amplifiers and speakers carefully concealed.

For those who can't have too much bling – this is your thing. The only limit to a total rebuild such as this is imagination and how much chrome you can afford. 'Bad 54' logo is stitched into the seats and panels.

Paint, chrome, toys and more chrome than you could ever imagine – it's simply excess all areas. Not a car for the shy retiring type.

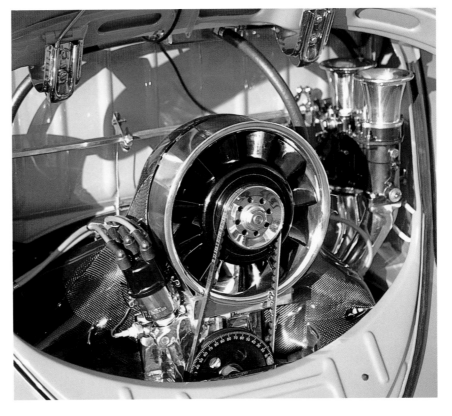

2 Cool 4 School

THE OBJECT of this exercise usually provokes two distinct reactions: outright approval from those who get the joke or abject horror for those who view it as a desecrated 21-window Samba. Whatever your opinion, this is one weird VW conversion. It may not be the world's first shortened Samba, nor the first chopped and lowered, but it may just be the first to be chopped and shortened. Its history is somewhat uncertain but it seems it first appeared at a VW drag meet at Irwindale, California in 2002 painted green with polished five-spoke alloys. Responsibility for the radical conversion job was placed at the door of one 'Uncle Bondo' who resides in Los Angeles. He obviously relished a challenge for he removed some two feet of metal from the wheelbase of a '66 Samba and chopped six inches from the roof. As a result, the windscreen post was canted back at an extreme angle and some custom wheel arches were fabricated. At the end of 2003, it passed to a new owner who discovered that it required a fair bit of work to get it back into shape. After many beers, the suggestion that it should be turned into a school bus seemed like a good idea, since interior space was no longer what it was and a mini-Samba has to be ideal. Running gear is generally stock, but the 1835cc engine with dual 44 Webers can raise the lowered front end during full-power starts from the lights.

Honey – they shrunk the Bus! This chopped, shortened and lowered Bus makes it the world's most child-friendly VW and the perfect vehicle for the school run. It may be crazy, but it's fun!

The wheels seem to be in the right place but the body has been shrunk by 18 inches!

Thin Is In

VIEWED IN profile, it looks like a Beetle with a wild set of wide wheels mounted clear of the bodywork. Viewed head-on and you will wonder if the wacky-baccy is having a bad effect – but do not adjust your vision as this anorexic Bug really does look like that. In a crazy world of chopping and shortening all manner of VWs, it was inevitable that someone would make a thin one. If ever you wondered what would happen if you took an electric sabre saw and cut away 18 inches of sheet metal from the middle of your beloved Bug, now you know. This strange beast hails from California (you guessed) and the owner, with his own salvage yard on hand to supply parts, sliced a 1964 saloon in half and then very carefully welded the two sections back together, taking considerable time and care to ensure the roof line retained the correct shape. Naturally the floorpan also had to lose 18 inches, although the central backbone was retained. Inside, the pedals, steering wheel and driver and passenger seats were centrally located in the manner of a WWII fighter plane. The stock engine was retained but the creation obviously needed more power, so in went a Porsche 911 6-pot. This unit soon died, so a 1971 dual port four took its place to be more in keeping with the car and more reliable. This is no trailer queen as it gets used regularly and in the photographs it was in the middle of a 1500-mile round trip to the Bonneville Speed Week.

Things look almost normal in profile but it's when this anorexic Bug is viewed from the front or rear that things get slightly disturbing. By necessity, the steering is centrally mounted and the passenger sits directly behind the driver, in full fighter pilot mode – jolly good show!

Viva Mexico!

AS MOST people are aware, when VW in Germany decided it was the end of the line for the Peoples' Car, the announcement was only partly accurate since it was considered that the good folk of Mexico would still be interested in the car as affordable and reliable transport. In fact a great deal of VW production was transferred to the Puebla factory and the old Bug continued to roll off the production lines alongside the Golf and New Beetle. Rumours of production quality gremlins have always been around but close inspection points to a car at least as well built as any '70s Bug. The advantage of the Mexican car is that, for less money than a full restoration job, you can own a new car. In fact, the model was finally terminated at the end of 2004, but many nearly-new examples can still be found today. The car in the photographs is a 2001 model and came with a 1600cc engine. They also have multi-point fuel injection, three-way catalytic converter and electronic ignition. As a by-product, the ECU can be chipped to take advantage of the better quality fuel in the UK and this can produce up to 40 per cent more power! All cars come with disc brakes at the front but no servo. Standard equipment is quite impressive and includes items such as an alarm, velour trim and Golf-style reclining seats, sports steering wheel, side repeaters, lockable fuel cap and reversing lights. This example has been converted to rhd at the expense of the glovebox and numerous dealer-added items increased the spec, and price, considerably. It has been fully soundproofed and has metallic paint, anti-corrosion treatment, a CD player and a full external chrome trim kit.

This Bug started life in Mexico but arrived in the UK where the steering was converted across and all manner of accessories added.

Jean Genius

FOR THE benefit of everybody who thought an orange Bus just would not work, prepare to be corrected – orange Buses are cool! The example displayed for your delight and education is the second restoration it has experienced, but the first saw it finished in red oxide primer with a denim interior and lowered suspension. The paint job was 'different' but it had a scruffy appearance, not helped by the standard of fit and finish inside. When it came up for sale, an exchange was made with an Oval Beetle but it was soon discovered that a) it's very easy to wipe the bumpers off on speed humps and b) the body was held together with filler. Body restoration was the familiar story of the small hole that just got bigger and bigger. To the serious detriment of the credit card, most of the lower regions had new metal welded in, plus the window surrounds, headlights bowls and roof. Six months later, the bare metal Bus met with a quantity of Fiat burnt orange paint which certainly shows off the shape better than the original choice of colour, chocolate brown. All door handles were removed and the holes filled and a solenoid used to open the driver's door, the tailgate being operated via a hidden catch. Running gear includes the front beam of an early Bay Window, narrowed by three inches. At the rear, the straight axle has been lowered three clicks and Eagle 520 Centreline-style wheels with ultra-low profile tyres help keep the look of the Bus very low indeed. Inside, charity shops were raided to source 82 pairs of denims which were skilfully cut up and used to trim the entire interior, the back pockets being used for storage in the doors. Different!

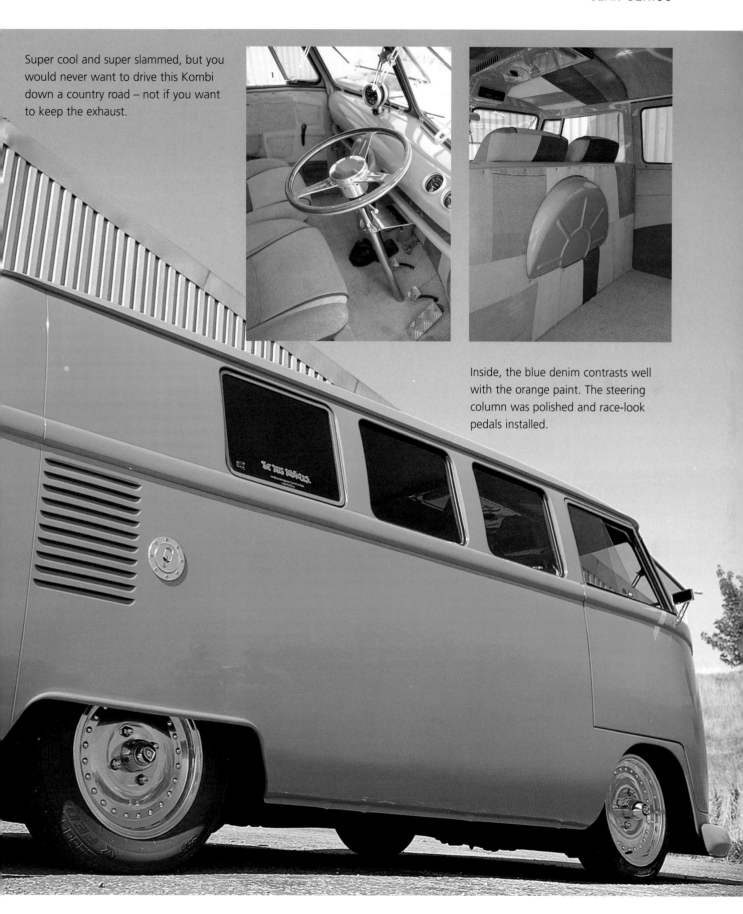

Super cool and super slammed, but you would never want to drive this Kombi down a country road – not if you want to keep the exhaust.

Inside, the blue denim contrasts well with the orange paint. The steering column was polished and race-look pedals installed.

Dream Car

ONE OF the most popular colours for a restored Ghia is silver and it hardly requires an excuse to publish more pictures, just to prove the point. This 1964 Karmann was imported into the UK from San Francisco and purchased by its new owner as a prelude to ownership of his dream car, a Porsche 356. The Ghia would serve as a taste of delights to come, so money was transferred and the neat, tidy car was his. It seemed solid enough, so there was little need for concern as it served as everyday transport. However, the replacement 1500cc engine seemed lacking in the performance department and became a cause for concern. The good news was that the engine was fine; the bad news was that is turned out to be a 1200cc lump. Then the speedo cable snapped and electrical gremlins struck. A visit to a VW specialist helped improve the running problems and, at the same time, the ride height was lowered to improve the looks and motorway stability. Then one of those annoying 5mph impacts with a solid object caused £2000 worth of body damage. It was back to the specialist where it was discovered that the solid bodywork was anything but. The repair work quickly became a full restoration project with the whole of the front end, floorpan, wings, inner and outer sills, rear quarter panel, engine bay and bulkhead, to name but a few items, all receiving attention. Over a year went by before the Ghia received its coat of diamond silver paint and several layers of lacquer. The engine was stripped and detailed before it was returned, along with new heat exchangers and exhaust, while a local coach trimmer renovated the interior and a vintage Blaupunkt Bremen radio completed the job.

This beautiful ex-resident of San Francisco flattered to deceive since it was not the sound, reliable automobile that it appeared to be. Once the bank balance had recovered from an unexpected battering, the full-on restoration looks well worth all the time and effort spent on it.

Surprise Surprise

YOU MAY think this is simply a beautifully restored, gently customized Oval that rides on a set of 17 inch Porsche Turbo 4 alloys. That's essentially correct but look closer and you will see that it is much, much more than that. Almost four years of hard labour went into this car to create a VW with supercar performance, capable of being used on the street or drag strip. Its owner is a fabricator with Autocad knowledge – an essential skill for anyone undertaking such a major project. The story began with a '56 Oval in very poor condition. Naturally every nut and bolt was removed and the search for parts began; the rear deck lid came from Sweden while the bonnet was found in Australia. With serious performance in mind, brakes were cannibalized from a Porsche 944S. In fact a great deal of hardware was sourced from Porsche, even the 924 seats, retrimmed in grey leather. 25mm torsion bars stop the car digging in too hard under heavy acceleration while custom-built coilover shock absorbers allow the suspension to be fine-tuned. A great deal of the car is custom built, even the home made drilled aluminium gear shift. But the heart of the matter was the engine and a monster Type 4 was planned. This started with a Type 4 crankcase from a 1700cc engine, carefully machined, and a 74mm stroke crank was bolted to a set of stock conrods with raceware bolts. To allow for a turbocharger, the cam choice was on the mild side and compression ratio kept low at 7.8:1. The result was a 2466cc unit bolted to a Garrett T35 turbo that produced 270bhp at 5000rpm, capable of a 13.02 second quarter-mile, with more to come.

Big wheels + big engine = big performance. In fact, a big boy's toy, built without compromise.

They don't make Beetles like this any more – and they never did. Well, they made the '56 bodyshell and chassis but under the skin this beautiful restoration is more Porsche than VW.

Das Kool Bulli

THERE IS a certain style about a 1953 23-window Barndoor Bus and this example was saved from its life as an unloved, pimped-out '80s Cal-Look by an owner who crossed the North American continent in a pick-up and returned with it to his home in Florida. He had photographed the Bus on an earlier Californian pilgrimage to the renowned VW Classic weekend, before seeing it for sale on the internet some time later. Close inspection revealed it was dry and rot-free, so money changed hands and it was hauled 3000 miles to begin a new life on the opposite coast. It was originally a Deluxe model but not many original bits remained, so the search began and a two-year rebuild to original specification got under way. Out came all the airplane cockpit-style toggle switches, Perspex accessories and wall-to-wall shag carpet to be replaced with new old stock parts such as the rear bumper, reflectors, lighter, starter button, popout latches, fuel reserve valve, correct speedometer and clock, plus an original Telefunken radio. Some original Plexiglas skylight and corner windows were unearthed and every part rechromed. It was decided to lower the Bus by using a Type 1 swing axle that slips in and bolts up. Rear discs were added by way of a Porsche 914, but the suspension remained standard. It now rides on Sears Radar sport wheels with Continental tyres and the Bus now enjoys life as a daily driver in the Sunshine State.

A trip from California to Florida resulted in this beautiful restoration to a 1953 Barndoor Bus. Underneath the red oxide primer was a sound vehicle that only required the dents hammering out. The after market front 'bumper' is decidedly different and affords highly effective protection.

Clockwork Orange

THIS CLASSIC Manx Buggy has been built with all the correct bits and pieces, with Gene Berg's name on the manifolds and Claude's Buggies on the valve covers. However, when you discover that the owner of this little gem restores antique clocks for a living, you just know that the beauty will be more than skin deep. Crawl around the nooks and crannies and you will discover unrivalled attention to detail. It so nearly all went wrong at one stage, when the original Vulture Buggy was acquired in 1989 and served for only two years before it became obvious that major surgery would be required to keep it safe and road legal. On closer inspection, it was discovered that the floorpan was of 1947 vintage. Sadly, having been chopped and shortened, it had no value to a restorer, but still had some value as the oldest basis for any Buggy. When the Vulture was stripped to its bones, the scale of the project proved somewhat daunting and the car languished for eight years until a friend offered to rebuild it for free (which is, of course, what friends are for). Armed with an advert for Mel Hubbard's run of Meyers Manx 2 bodies, they inspected the product and ordered an orange tub. The task of renovating the '47 floorpan then got under way. The brakes were overhauled with Goodridge stainless braided hoses and the 57-year old shocks replaced with EMPI versions. The original, highly prized 1994cc engine was built in the States and is crowned with modified 'Berg Special' Weber 44DCNFs, worked on by the late Mr. Berg himself. In the world of Buggies, it gets no better than this.

It may look like a simple, basic buggy but every area shows huge attention to detail and craftsmanship – very cool.

There's more than one way to skin a cat and more than one way to build a Manx – Custom, Race, Hi-Tech or Classic, as with this orange gem. It's an object lesson in buggy building.

Gran Turismo

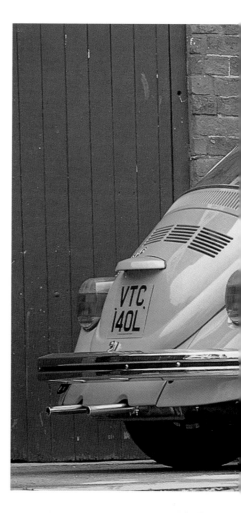

THE 1973 GT Beetle is the factory special edition which, in the eyes of most Volkswagen enthusiasts, was the dream Beetle. The model had the best features and attributes available, such as a 1584cc 50 horsepower motor linked to a higher final drive swing axle transmission. This was to be the largest capacity engine fitted to any Beetle and, with that gearbox, it was also the fastest. The 1584cc engine was offered in the 1302S and later in the 1303S, but the GT was the only flat screen German Beetle to be equipped with this engine. The GT was special in other areas. It came with the 4.5 inch steel sports wheels that became known as GT wheels. The rear wings were the 1303-style wings with big 'elephants' foot' rear lights. The rest of the exterior was the same as a normal flat screen, but big rear lights and wheels aside, you'd never miss a GT Beetle on the street as they were painted in one of three very lurid colours: lemon yellow (as this example), apple green and tomato red. Interestingly, the GT Beetle differed from any other Beetle as it actually had the word 'Beetle' on the back of the car. The 'GT Beetle' deck lid badge wasn't actually factory fitted, but dealer fitted. The factory badge applied to the 2500 UK examples was '1300S', but Volkswagen GB replaced them with their own chrome-plated plastic badges. A GT can still be found but, as with most VWs from the mid-'70s, they tend to rot – this example required major restoration to 'as new' condition, but for the cost of a used GT plus circa £10,000, it still makes a sensible and economical choice.

The 'Gran Turismo' of the Beetle world will always be a highly desirable model for those who enjoy driving. This pristine example has drilled window winders and an elegant Flat Four 'GTV' steering wheel.

Arachnophobia

ONE OF the joys of 'restoring' a rotten VW Beetle is that, with a little imagination and a modest amount of cash, it can be morphed into that other doyen of the air-cooled philosophy – a Porsche. In this case, a truly rough donor car of '68 vintage allowed its chassis to be shortened and gently modified before being united with a GP kit of glass fibre panels in the shape of the classic Porsche 718 RSK. Thus the humble Bug returned to the road in the guise of a lightweight two-seat sports car that offers the ultimate wind-in-the-hair motoring experience. An essential element in creating such a vehicle is to get the ride and handling sorted; the front beam was modified with the aid of a Sway-A-Way adjuster in the top tube and the smaller adjuster leaves removed from the bottom tube. This leaf removal had the effect of reducing the spring rate of the front suspension, lowering the vehicle and softening the ride – just what is needed with such a lightweight bodyshell. Brakes were sourced from a '67 Bug, chosen for their wide five-lug stud pattern as used on the original Spyder and the same car donated its slotted wheels that are also similar to those used on the Porsche. Naturally, the engine had to deliver the goods and a tired old 1600cc was hardly suitable. A 1914cc Type 1 motor was built around a counterweighted 69mm crank, lightweight flywheel and a lumpy Engle 125 cam. At tickover, the engine burbles and pops, but past 3500rpm it delivers the power! The ensemble was set off with a stratos silver paint job, Moto-Lita steering wheel and a set of replica seats with full harness belts.

Thanks to a thumping 1914cc motor, this Spyder is as scary as they come! This authentic-looking, very fast 'replica' of a Porsche 718RSK was created from a tatty £300 Bug.

Hit the Beach

THE GOOD people of California have always enjoyed a close
relationship with the Beetle. The car was the perfect antidote to the
excessive vehicles that rolled out of Detroit during the '60s and '70s;
twenty feet long, seven feet wide with chrome everywhere. The Beetle
occupied a rarefied space at the other end of the spectrum and those who
appreciated them, rushed to buy. In time, many were scrapped but the
custom car community took the quirky little car to its heart and thereby
saved many VWs from their inevitable fate. When a small ad in *The
Recycler* magazine (the equivalent of the UK's *Autotrader*) for a 1962
Karmann Beetle was spotted by a long-term VW fanatic he rushed off to
inspect the vehicle and returned home with his prize. It lacked front
wings, hood, interior, window frames or glass, the roof was in poor
condition and rust had attacked the rear end. But such minor irritations
aside, the basic essentials existed for a full four year Cal-Look restoration
that returned this classic Beetle to the road and a new lease of life. The
owner lives in Pomona, the site of one of the largest swap meets in
California, so sourcing parts was not much of a problem. The bodywork
was sprayed with a serious amount of paint, a 1914cc motor installed and
a set of chrome-plated EMPI five-spoke alloy wheels set the whole thing
off. The interior has been trimmed to perfection in shades of tan and
beige. The cloth-centred door panels have been perforated since they
contain the speakers for the cleverly concealed modern sound system.
The correct period radio mounted in the dash is purely for authenticity.

Four and a half years work resulted in
this immaculate cool Cal Convertible.
The sparkling 1914cc engine was
finished to show-car quality;
photographs fail to do justice
to the perfect interior.

Sunshine Bus

W HEN VW ceased production of the Split-screen, we lost forever the Deluxe Microbus, or Samba as it was known. Although it did not gain the same legendary status as its older brother, the Bay-window Deluxe became the new Samba. The Deluxe Microbus wasn't the best selling Type 2 Transporter in the UK by any stretch of the imagination as, when this Bus was new, the British public was more interested in buying the Campers, or Caravanettes as many people referred to them. These were converted by companies such as Devon. Thus the market for the Minibus was small and many were purchased in basic form, so to find an example such as this 1972 Bus that was fitted from new with a steel sliding roof is rare indeed – possibly unique. When purchased in 1997, it was obvious that a fair amount of effort would be required to return it to its original glory. In 1999, it was obvious that the work would have to be carried out sooner rather than later, but when the paint was stripped off, the news was far from good. On the plus side, the near rear-side corner was OK but other than that, enough new metal was grafted on to restore the Forth Bridge. New doors were sourced and after many moons in a specialist workshop it finally emerged with a new red and white paint job. It was then down to a good cleaning and restoration of the interior, the addition of a period roof rack and a set of Type 2-pattern BRM replica wheels to set it all off; plus some very expensively chromed bumpers of course.

This Deluxe had acquired a host of extras – wheels, bumpers, step, roofrack, windows, lights to name but a few. The interior *(opposite)* is beautifully renovated with all the right bits; the Type 2 stud-pattern BRM replica wheels look very racy; the sliding sunroof is a very rare option.

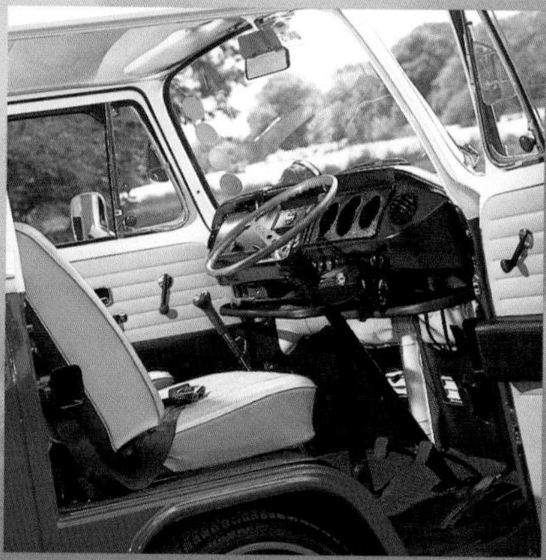

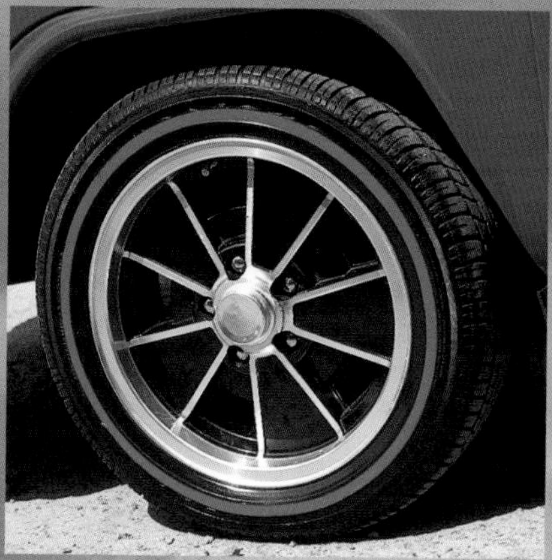

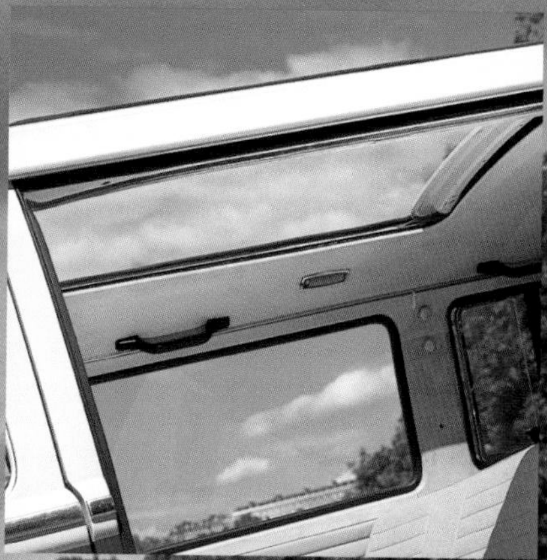

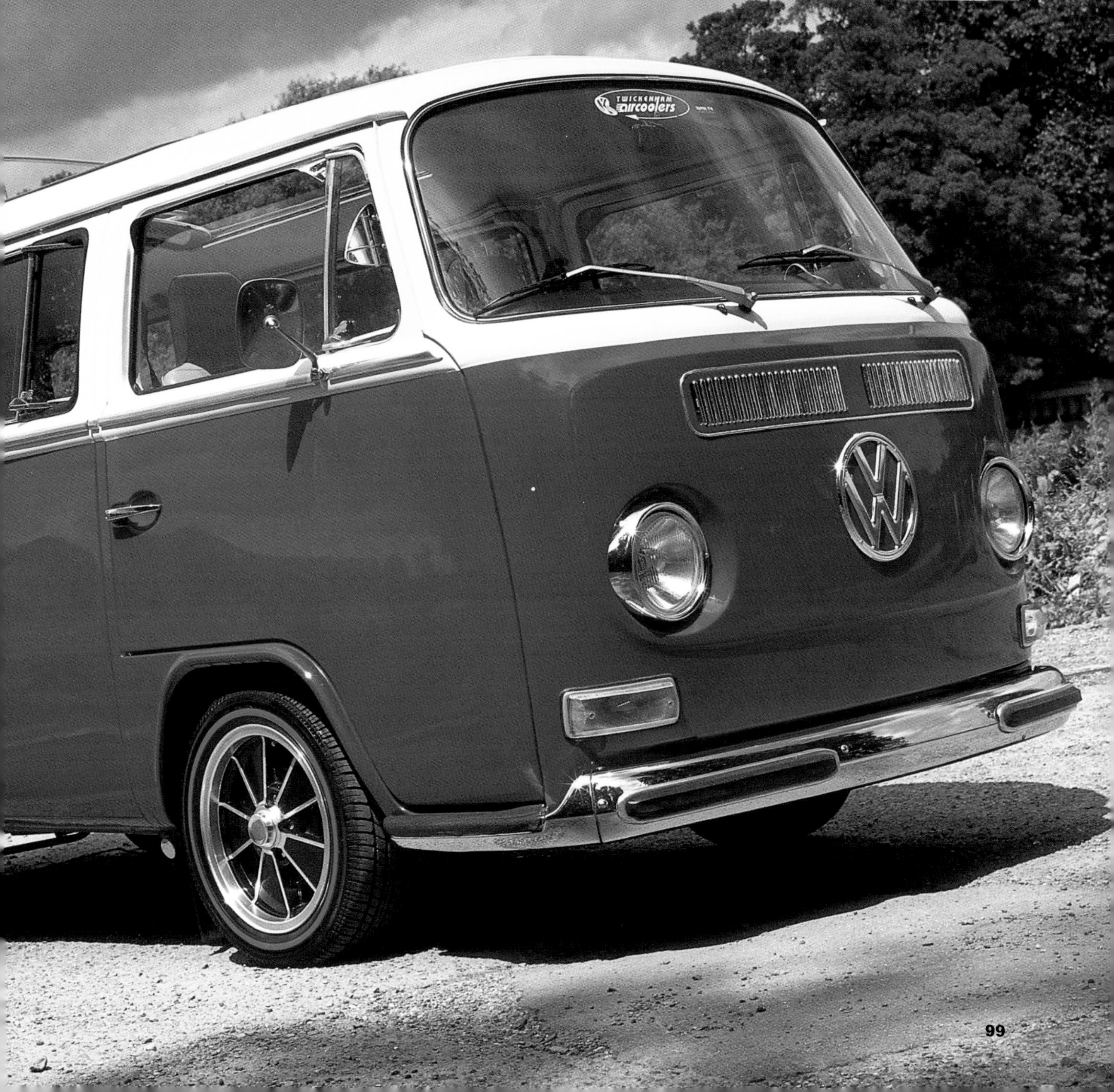
TWICKENHAM
aircoolers

The Right Stuff

If you plan to build a serious Beetle for the street, this is your target. It's every bit as hard as it looks with serious performance on tap. BBS parts are everywhere – wheels, seats and steering wheel with carbon fibre inserts, plus carbon fibre on the dash.

THERE'S MORE to this modified Bug than an eye-searing green paintjob and a set of serious wheels – but while we are on the subject, the BBS alloys really do give the car a certain presence! They are 17-inch RS2 splitrims wrapped in low-profile Yokohama rubber and the paint is L62Y gift green, Having established all that – what about the rest? The basis of this German-Look Beetle was a 1984 Bug from Mexico and it was given the full treatment by Remmele Motorsports in France. They installed a set of wide wheel arches to accommodate the wheels and carried the BBS component theme into the cockpit with a smart carbon-trimmed steering wheel and high-back BBS seats. Remmele built the engine around a Type 4 case with a stock 71mm crank and 94mm barrels and pistons to give 1971cc, fed via a pair of 44mm IDF carbs. When the 319 degree cam finally kicks in, it pulls forever and helps the car disappear down the road with unseemly haste. It sounds very impressive inside the car since the firewall has no soundproofing, just a coat of gift green paint. It has to be said that the engine bay looks impressive with a Porsche cooling fan and alternator, all wrapped in a beautiful custom-built carbon-fibre fan housing. To cope with the three-fold increase in power, the ride height has been dropped and the stock dampers replaced with Bilstein units, so it can corner as impressively as it shifts in a straight line. When the owner tires of the sound of the twin-choke carbs, he can dial up Kraftwerk on the Pioneer KEH-P62000 sound system as he blasts along the Deutsche autobahns.

Karmann Chameleon

WHEN A Karmann Ghia falls into the hands of a Hot Rod fan (and a skilled aircraft engineer to boot) you just know that when the restoration job is finished, something very different and wonderful will emerge from his garage. This Ghia is no exception and it featured some beautiful engineering touches, such as the customized dashboard that contains just three large dials found at a Hot Rod swap meet, and all the minor switch gear transferred to a simple, elegant curved sheet of metal located on the central tunnel, complete with 'phone cradle. All customized Karmanns are unique in their own way, but the feature of this car that grabs the attention is the paintwork. Sadly, it is all but impossible to convey the effect in two dimensions as the colour changes from green to purple as the car, or your viewing angle, moves and it changes dramatically in different lighting conditions. It is one colour in sunlight, changes when it becomes overcast and is different again at night. If you need to ask how much the DuPont paint costs, you can't afford it, but the effect is undoubtedly worth the expense. This Ghia was imported from the States in poor condition and went downhill from there. A front-end shunt dictated that the nose had to be reformed on an English wheel (a dying art) and the floorpan was rotten – hardly surprising since one half of it turned out to be an ex-American road sign! This proves that not everyone knows how to restore a car. After considerable time and money, the car was sprayed and the engine and boot areas finished in gold paint. The interior was beautifully retrimmed in green and grey tweed cloth, topped off with a bat-wing steering wheel from an early Oval Beetle.

The finest blue-green-purple-gold Ghia you will ever see, courtesy of a remarkable paint job from Du Pont. Very weird, but wonderful!

When Hot Rod skills are applied to a Karmann Ghia coupe, the result will be different and interesting. The quality of craftsmanship is exemplary. Wheels came from a VW Trekker (!) and the steering wheel was sourced from an Oval and sprayed pearl metallic white.

Cool Water

IN THE case of this very highly modified 1964 Devon Camper, it would be best to get its dark secret out into the open from the off – it's water cooled! Naturally such heresy is usually punishable by ten years of Lada ownership, but a close inspection of the quality of this conversion will win over even the most hardened VW-ist. It also serves to explain the odd front bumper with a hole in it as a radiator had to be installed under the cab floor at an angle with the heater installed in the cab, behind the front seats. The water pipes were fabricated from galvanized steel and routed through the chassis rails, cooling the 1.8-litre motor from an Audi 80 Sport. A stainless steel exhaust system with a Lotus Elise backbox exits from the centre of the rear bumper. It was decided to run the Bus as low as possible and this was achieved by fabricating new wheel arches that extend higher into the cab for additional clearance. The cab doors were converted to 'suicide' spec, being rear hinged, and all external handles and assorted items were deleted. A complete independent rear suspension was donated from a 1303S Super Beetle, while the fuel tank received a swirl pot and return lines for the Bosch K-Jetronic fuel injection system. The white-over-yellow paintjob continued inside and underneath the 'shell and tinted windows were cut to size. Inside the Bus has been converted into a playroom and chillout lounge with a Playstation, TV and drinks cabinet, plus full Sony sound system. Dozens of Fiat side-repeater lights installed around the roof give the desirable 'candle-lit' effect at night.

Giving a very good impression of a
hovercraft when seen from the front on
the road, this unique Devon Bus really
does have wheels, plus a trick in the tail
– a water-cooled engine from an Audi
80, which explains the slot in the front
bumper. Suicide doors give the Bus a
Batmobile look!

Bhp Central

OK YOU think – it's another fairly stock, fancy silver Beetle running on Porsche 993 alloys to give it a bit of street cred. Big deal. But hold on, the secret of this little monster lies somewhere south of the rear alloys, for bolted firmly in place out back is a wild 2.8-litre motor mated to a truly awesome turbocharger. The result of this remarkable bit of plumbing is a gearbox-munching power output of 525bhp at 18psi – in a street legal Bug! If you ever come across this fearsome creature while tooling around the Simi Valley in California, do the right thing and let it past. No point in trying to outrun it. The owner of the car came into possession of the engine after sensibly keeping it as security for a debt. When the cash was not forthcoming, the engine became his property. This decidedly special flat-four unit, built by Autocraft, is considered capable of producing 800bhp at a massive 45psi – not that it has ever been turned up that high since it had over $20,000 invested in it. It was originally built for use in an off-road Buggy (or sand-rail, in SoCal parlance) but its proud new owner thought it might be more fun in the back of his Oval-window '56 Bug. While he was at it he added a full-length sunroof but kept the dash and steering wheel standard (funny guy) but added the necessary extra instrumentation. The rear seats were ditched and the rear luggage area was boxed in to cover the huge turbocharger that sits above the gearbox and runs with two wastegates, as they can only handle 450bhp each! A huge rollcage keeps everything rigid, but acceleration from 50mph in third is Space Shuttle quick and, running on methanol, dumps the fuel at a wallet-shrinking rate of two and a half miles per gallon. So there you are – this is not a stock Beetle.

If power corrupts, this Bug would corrupt absolutely! No 45bhp 1956 Oval ever went down the road so quickly and no doubt, no other '56 will. A very special and expensive engine with twin wastegates and 525bhp on tap *(far left)*. In place of the rear seats, a huge turbocharger sits above the gearbox *(left)*.

Occasionally, an opportunity arises to buy a one-owner Beetle but you need to be ready with cash in your hand. This example was lovingly garaged every night, although a respray was required after 40 years of Californian sunshine.

Counting Coppers

THIS MUCH-loved Beetle came into ownership of a retired police officer in California after a long campaign of polite persistence aimed at its first owner, a librarian. She purchased the car in Colorado in 1967 while at university and it stayed with her when she returned to Hawaii and, several years later, to California. She carefully maintained the car during their thirty year partnership, by which time it had accumulated 145,000 miles with one engine rebuild at 125,000. When the time came to part company, the Volkswagen-loving policeman responded to her 'phone call within the hour and the Bug was finally his. All that was required was a little light restoration and some new German-sourced rubber trim and it was fit to become his everyday road car, clocking up another 40,000 miles during the first five years in his company. The '67 model is still considered very desirable since it was the last of the 'original' cars, before a number of changes were introduced with the 1968 models. By 1967, the Beetle was pretty much sorted, with a heater that worked tolerably well, the seats were comfortable, door seals were tight and the general workings of the power train had reached their production-quality pinnacle. With its larger windows, improved lights and more rear seat space it was a substantial improvement on earlier models in terms of quality and practicality. During 1968, some 1300 Beetles were imported into the USA with the 1493cc flat-four and a 12-volt system as standard, but still with drum brakes instead of the discs used in other countries. The '68 cars arrived with such innovations as a collapsible steering column, new fuel system, new suspension with double-jointed rear axle on some models and optional 'tombstone' seats that heralded the advent of a new generation of Beetle.

Split Screen Angels

ANY CAR that achieves a certain level of popularity inevitably attracts one or two unscrupulous characters who will jump onto any bandwagon if they smell the chance of making a financial killing. The surge in the popularity of the humble Beetle during the late '80s saw a sudden increase in the numbers of so-called 'restoration experts'. Not that every one was a cowboy operator by any means, but not all had honourable intentions and many customers got their fingers burnt. The same thing appears to be happening now with Split-screen Buses as numerous 'celebrities' and folk with cash to spare search around for a suitable example to add to their collection. To feed this demand, more specialist restorers come out of the woodwork. However, it's no easy task finding a suitable Bus; do you buy a fully restored example and pray it's not a 'chicken wire and filler' special or do you buy an untouched original example, running the risk of discovering serious rot, since these large commercial vehicles spend most of their lives in the open air. But once in a while, when the Split angels are smiling, a clean original example can still be found. This one was spotted by a smart kid from the window of a school bus, parked alongside a house. His father was informed, he got excited, money changed hands and the old black and grey paint was stripped to uncover the Holy Grail – a genuine rot-free Bus, *sans* accident damage. A good clean and a respray in VW zenith blue and white brought this unmolested Bus back to life.

Who could pass up the opportunity to buy a genuine, rot-free Split-screen Bus such as this? The original interior was shabby, but plenty of soap and water soon resolved that problem.

21st Century Toy

IT WAS not so long ago that the possibility of anyone building a relatively stock-looking Beetle capable of returning quarter-mile drag strip times circa 12 seconds was considered the stuff of dreams. Now, thanks to the massive VW aftermarket industry, such fantasies are a real possibility as this '66 Cal-Look Beetle can confirm, with its 12.19 timing ticket safely in its glovebox. In the mid-1970s, the newly coined term 'Cal-Look' referred specifically to a certain type of car that emerged from the workshops around Orange County, Los Angeles. The expression was later applied to anything that had been lowered but today, a Cal-Look car has to be much more than that, as illustrated by this awesome creation. This is far more than just another paint job and shiny wheels, as it has undergone the full Cal-Look treatment by being stripped to the last nut and bolt and reassembled with near-fanatical attention to detail. The nuts and bolts themselves are either correctly detailed originals or stainless steel replacements and the floorpan was cleaned, painted, powder coated, polished and detailed. Looking inside the car, many people would consider it pretty much stock, with standard steering wheel and seats, but the give-away features are the Autometer tach, the Berg shifter and black Simpson lap belts. When the engines fires, it is instantly apparent that this is not a stock motor as the 2276cc flat-four barks into life, fed by twin 48IDA Webers. This ultimate powerhouse has never been dynoed but the drag strip times tell the story – that and the fact that it can be driven on the road!

Fancy sports and woodrim wheels
(above) are no longer de rigeur –
original wheels always look right.
The engine of a Cal-Looker (left) is the
single most important ingredient; twin
48IDAs and ultra-detailed stroker-
motors remain the defining feature.

Import Export

THEY SAY that every cloud has a silver lining and for this once-tired and grubby Beetle, an unfortunate fire that saw the demise of a Type 2 camper resulted in two distraught owners set off in search of another set of VW-shaped wheels. A small ad in the back of an issue of *VolksWorld* offered a very original red '59 Beetle with just two owners from new. A visit to the vendor revealed a very tired and decidedly grubby, uncared-for Beetle that appeared sound and genuine. The deal was done and the car now faced a happier future. A little research into its history revealed that it had been built at Wolfsburg on November 14th 1959 and exported to Columbia but for some unexplained reason had been shipped to the UK in 1962. Colborne Garages then sold it to a German gentleman who lived and worked in Britain and he kept the car for 32 years, covering 120,000 miles. The task of reviving the Beetle began badly when it was taken to a local garage. In seven months they succeeded in stripping off the paint and leaving it parked outside to deteriorate further. Naturally the car was reclaimed and sent to another restorer where the car was repainted in the original shade of Indian red. Finances dictated that a lot of the work was carried out at home and the wheels were finished in the original colour scheme of black and grey, an option on 1959 export models. An exterior sun visor was sourced from Germany but the finishing touch came in the form of a very desirable period supercharger that gives this very original-looking '59 car the performance of a 1600cc twin-port motor.

At first glance, this could be taken for a nicely restored '60s Beetle with whitewall tyres until you spot the semaphore indicators that confirm it to be a late '50s model. The interior is faultless and beautiful period accessories are everywhere, right down to the correct Judson supercharger.

Summer Fun

THERE ARE, as you know, Buggies that are built right and quite a few that are built wrong! Displayed before you is a Buggy that was initially very wrong but with a little tender loving care, has been properly 'righted'. As it were. This is one of those purchases from the pages of *Exchange & Mart* that saved a truly unloved MkI GP Buggy from its inevitable demise, The gearbox was of a mid-sixties vintage so it did not bolt on to the '54 Oval floorpan properly, so somebody had cut the bodywork so that the nose cone sat on top of the floorpan tunnel with the shift rod bent up through the inspection hole in an effort to line up with the nose cone. Also, the bodywork was full of holes that had been drilled to accommodate various accessories and the dash had been badly molested and covered in brown vinyl! So – plenty of room for improvement in most departments. In went a later model pedal cluster and handbrake mechanism along with new brake pipes throughout, plus the addition of five-bolt drums on the rear for better stopping. When the body went back on, everything was sanded back to the glass fibre and the central instrument cluster was relocated in front of the driver and the dash modified accordingly. To overcome the Buggy problem of having the steering wheel in an awkward place, the steering column was shortened and lowered. The bodywork received three coats of primer and three of Vauxhall yellow before the custom roll cage was finally installed, finished in a contrasting shade of lilac.

For those who crave a classic Beetle or Bus, but whose bank balance seems to contain a black hole into which cash seems mysteriously drawn, a humble buggy may just be the answer to your prayers in the never-ending search for affordable fun.

Wide Boy

LUCKILY, THE VW resto scene is one that is constantly evolving, which means that every so often a brave owner will accept a self-imposed challenge to create something new and exciting. Inevitably, those who dare break out of the mould run the risk of criticism from the more 'traditional' people who like to keep things the way they are, but evolution will always find a way as this Bus demonstrates. When this custom Bay arrived on the show circuit, a few eyebrows were raised. The first thing that grabs the attention is, naturally, the paintwork, a House of Kolors Chameleon six-colour paint. The application of purple, blue, gold, green, bronze and cyan took two weeks to apply and the colours change as you move around the Bus, where you also discover some radical rear wheel arches. These were custom-built using the original arch plus a little extra sheet metal. Why are they there? Because nobody had done it before. Big wheels were always on the agenda and the 18x7.5-inch Lenson Spinners (with free rotating outer trim) certainly fill the arches and are shod with Pneumant rubber. At the rear, a Perspex hatch gives a clear view of the chromed engine bay. The body was stripped of door handles, with a solenoid taking care of the opening and closing, including the gull-wing side door. No boring side-hinged metalwork here – this one is top-hinged and lifts with the aid of a 24-volt electric ram. Once inside, all is black with silver highlights and cushions (plus the obligatory pimps' cane). The sound system is huge and loud with countless LED lights recessed into the headlining. Please do not ask what all this craftsmanship and labour cost, but the result is one seriously different Bus.

Building a Bus to this standard is no easy task. Time, money, a wild imagination and single-minded dedication are just some of the requirements needed to achieve this level of perfection.

Leader of the Pack

BEING THE president of a VW Club brings with it many
responsibilities, not least of which is – what VW do you drive?
Naturally, others in your club will look to you for leadership and
guidance, so turning up in a ratty '60s beetle or run of the mill Split is
scarcely the thing. Fortunately for the president of the Limburgse
Keverclub in Belgium, he can lay claim to being only the second owner
of this 1953 Oval Beetle. It was found at a VW dealership that was
closing its doors in 1997. The garage had not bothered to register it after
taking it in part exchange for a new VW some 40 years earlier. Luckily it
had been stored in a dry heated garage and had only covered 94,403km
in the hands of its original owner, but it was still considered advisable to
carry out a full renovation to ensure it survived another half century at
least. The body was carefully separated from the floorpan and these were
stripped to the bare metal and powder coated. The 25bhp 1131cc engine
still ran perfectly, but was stripped and treated to fresh piston rings
before reassembly, along with a new clutch. The only notable rust was
found at the lower edge of the passenger door and one rear quarterpanel.
These areas were carefully repaired and the body stripped before being
restored with several coats of atlantic green paint. The VW factory put
the owner in touch with the factory that supplied the material for the
interior in 1953 and they were able to supply enough fabric to retrim the
whole interior, including the rear bolster cushions. The Oval is now
proudly displayed at shows around Europe after its very sympathetic
three-year restoration.

This superb '53 Oval comes packed
with rare and desirable goodies such
as the classic batwing steering
wheel and rear seat cushions. The
ultra-rare and seriously expensive
glass washer-fluid bottle *(far right)* is
typical of the attention to detail
lavished on this classic.

Even a humble Single cab
benefits from a little tender
loving care, as this '63 demonstrates.
A sympathetic restoration can work wonders!

'63 and Single

IN ALL honesty, a drop-side pickup is rarely anyone's ride of choice but, if you are a builder or landscape gardener and haul paving slabs and half a ton of concrete for a living, you might as well travel in some degree of style. Therefore this VW single cab may just be the wheels of your dreams, even if you haven't realized it yet. This beautiful piece of custom work hails from Costa Mesa, California and is based on an $1800 disaster-master. A mere two months of dedicated work saw it revived and running, resplendent in a brilliant Porsche guards red paint scheme and a perfect interior trimmed in tan vinyl and tweed upholstery. This being California, in went a Sony 10-disc CD sound system, plus a Le Carra steering wheel, Gene Berg shifter and Dynomat sound insulation. However, this was no impulse buy as the owner had spent many years quietly acquiring all the necessary bits and pieces to carry out this conversion, always assuming that the right vehicle would come his way. This helped save considerable time sourcing parts as they were all ready and waiting. Underneath, a Bus Boys lowering kit provided the ride height of choice and was teamed up with KYB shocks all round with Gas-a-Just at the rear. Engine-wise the original 1600cc unit was completely rebuilt. A set of polished Porsche alloy wheels with 145 tyres up front and165 rear, added that extra touch of class. This just has to be the ultimate way to arrive at your local builder's merchant.

Muller Love

NOBODY IS certain how many Type 14A Hebmuller cabriolets were built between 1949 and 1953 and even fewer can say how many still survive today. According to Hebmuller, fewer than 700 were sold and it seems that around 50 survive, so these are amongst the rarest and most collectable of all Volkswagens. The Hebmuller story began during the British occupation of the VW works following WWII. Sir Ivan Hirst commissioned a special two-seater roadster for his boss, Colonel Charles Radclyffe and this car is thought to be the inspiration for the Hebmuller design, following a visit from Karmann and Hebmuller representatives who toured the factory while bidding for a contract to build cabriolets. Hebmuller won the two-seater contract with a design similar to the Radclyffe roadster, while Karmann were asked to build four-seater models. The first car was delivered on July 1st 1949 and work progressed well until a factory fire devastated the under-insured company a few weeks later on July 23rd. 358 cars were built that year but the company was in a financial mess, closing its doors in 1952. Karmann finished the remaining bodies in 1953 and that was the end of the Type 14A. The 1950 model in the photographs is one of the finest examples in the world since it is period-perfect in every way. It was purchased and stripped in 1995 and sent to Deanos Body Works in Tempe where 18 months was spent just ensuring the body was totally straight before it was painted with four coats of Spies Hecker black and burgundy. NOS parts were sourced from around the world and even such rarities as cable brakes and lever-arm shocks were unearthed. Every piece on the car, from the cross-ply tyres to the Telefunken radio, is correct and perfect in every way, making this a very valuable VW indeed!

Wonderful period details are to be found everywhere on this Type 14A Hebmuller convertible. The owner spent many years gathering a collection of NOS parts, down to the rear-view mirror with a small circular clock mounted above it. The dashboard features a restored Telefunken radio and glovebox cover. Larger '49 hubcaps were fitted simply because they looked right.

A Special Vintage

TO SECURE the Best Type 1 award at the *VolksWorld* Show is an indication that the car is the best in the UK. This elderly car won in 2003 but few will recall the fact, which is a minor tragedy for this Beetle is a gem in the huge world of Volkswagens since it dates back to October 19th 1948. It may be necessary to recall the situation back then; the war was over and the Wolfsburg factory was under the command of the British occupying forces. A young British major, Ivan Hirst, is credited with reversing the fortunes of Volkswagen after the war when he organized an inexperienced workforce to put Ferdinand Porsche's design into production to provide some form of transport within war-torn Europe. An order was agreed among the Allies to build 20,000 saloons and production resumed in 1946 even though it was clear that the necessary skills were lacking among the workers. Gradually production increased until, in October 1949, the factory returned to German ownership. What we have here is a 'British' VW (prior to 1949). These are difficult to restore accurately since few people knew what they looked like but, by a quirk of fate, this car was exported to

As if a '48 Beetle was not rare enough, this one features period-perfect items such as front and rear bumpers with 'banana' overriders, big logo hubcaps and correct ridged headlights with the VW logo at the bottom.

Czechoslovakia in 1953 and passed into the hands of one family until 1986. As soon as the Iron Curtain came down, a collector visited and discovered this totally original example. It had covered 500,000km and was running on a replacement engine – but the family still had the original! It also features the unique pressed steel dashboard and bumpers with 'banana' over-riders; in fact every part necessary to maintain this 'time-warp' classic in perfect original order.

'Ticka' reversing light doubles as a removable spotlight; 8-gallon fuel tank resides under the bonnet.